High Threshold Muscle Building

By Christian Thibaudeau

Editor: Tony Schwartz

F.Lepine Publishing
ISBN 978-1-4997660-7-3
2007 Publication
www.MuscleDriveThru.com

Table of Contents

INTRODUCTION
The High-Threshold training methodology 7

PRINCIPLE 1
Always try to generate as much force as possible 13

PRINCIPLE 2
Take advantage of the eccentric portion of a movement 19

PRINCIPLE 3
Precede the maximum concentric action by a prestretch of the muscle 27

PRINCIPLE 4
Training to the positive muscle failure point 35

PRINCIPLE 5
Including some plyometric work to train the nervous system 41

PRINCIPLE 6
Including a significant amount of unilateral work 47

PRINCIPLE 7
Including some unstable training to activate the nervous system 51

PRINCIPLE 8
Optimize the work-to-rest ratio 55

PRINCIPLE 9
Select the most effective exercises for each muscle group 63

PRINCIPLE 10
When trying to lose fat, add high-speed metabolic work 145

PRINCIPLE 11
Eccentric loading and deceleration training for strength, power and size ... 155

Exercises organisation 171

Bonus section: Isometric training 185

Parting words 199

Cool Tools, Equipment, Performance Store and Products that Coach Thib likes ... 201

About the Editor

Mike Hanley is a strength & conditioning coach based out of the East Coast of the United States. He is certified by USAW as a sports performance coach as well as a certified kettlebell instructor. Mike specializes in program design for high school athletes as well as middle aged men & women. His training methods include a mixture of powerliting, Olympic weightlifting, kettlebell training as well as many other methods to produce significant strength & performance gains. Mike has also worked closely with autistic teenagers as well as senior citizens both in the rehabilitative & fitness arena.

In addition to his work in the strength & conditioning field, Mike Hanley is also a competitive athlete. He has competed in bodybuilding, powerlifting, and weightlifting.

Mike Hanley is available for private training in the Marlboro, NJ and Belmar, NJ areas. In addition, Mike also designs personalized training, nutrition, and supplementation programs online. If you would like more information on Mike's programs please contact him at hanley.strength@gmail.com or visit www.hanleystrength.com.

INTRODUCTION
The High-Threshold training methodology

Upon reading the material contained in this new book some peoples might believe that I've finally come full circle. I originally started out exclusively as a performance coach, making my mark by introducing several innovative training methods to the strength-training world then switched to more of a bodybuilding focus; writing a book and some articles on that aspect of the iron game and training several athletes for physique contests. Those of you who are aware of my athletic training material will recognize several principles from this book and will quickly assume that I'm back to my roots. While this isn't entirely false, it isn't completely true either. Yes I'm back to a more "athletic" training optic, but I'm not back to where I started from; rather I'm still evolving as a coach and came to the realization that several principles that are applicable to athletic training can also be used to spark new muscle growth. The best way to describe this book would then to call it the "interracial" couple of aesthetics and athletics.

Everybody can take something out of this book: athletes will find new ways to improve their strength, power and metabolic efficiency. They will also learn how to build muscle that will be "usable" in their athletic endeavours. Bodybuilders will find out which are the best exercises for each muscle groups and will learn to apply athletic training principles to better be able to target the high-threshold motor units (HTMUs) which are the key to maximum muscle growth. Finally, the average trainee who wants to look good, lean and muscular but who also wants to be functional, healthy and fit will be able to apply the principles described to reach these objectives too. I'm not saying that everybody should train the same way. However I believe that there is some common ground to all forms of training, something rooted in science that can be applied by all to foster maximum growth and improvement regardless of the end objective.

Athletes and Bodybuilders both have some things right!

If you are reading this book chances are that:

a) You're looking for ways to improve your muscularity
b) You're looking for ways of losing body fat through training
c) You're looking for ways to become a more explosive athlete

d) You're looking for ways to get stronger

e) You're looking for sexy pictures of big bald Canadian coaches!

In fact a combination of all of these (except "e" I hope) objectives is probably what you're after. This is the mindset I was in when I sat down to write this book. If you apply the principles described in the following chapters you ***will*** gain muscle, lose fat, and become stronger, more explosive and more metabolically efficient. It's not the Holy Grail, but it is science properly applied to stimulate maximum body adaptation.

I said that some would think that I've gone full circle with this book. This might be true. Over the past decade or so I've been on both sides of the fence: I've trained and coached for strength and athleticism and for body transformation/bodybuilding too. At first I separated both approaches. Bodybuilding methods were in one drawer and strength/power methods in another one. When I worked with athletes I opened the "strength/power"drawer and took out what I needed; I did the same thing when designing bodybuilding workouts. Never had it crossed my mind that there might be something useful for bodybuilding development stored in the "strength/power" drawer and vice-versa. I've now learned to use stuff from both drawers. A training method or principle shouldn't be classified as a strength/power or bodybuilding method; you should keep an eye open to everything that might lead to the kind of gains you're looking for.

After all both athletes and bodybuilders give use clues: a lot of athletes have great bodies (muscular and lean) and a lot of bodybuilders are strong and powerful; yet both train radically different. This tells me that there is more than one way to skin a cat. Not only that, it also tells me that if we can combine the best principles of both worlds, we'll achieve the ideal body transformation methodology possible.

This is my objective with this book and hopefully I'll come somewhat close to that, you'll be the judge!

The 11 principles

Sadly I missed out on a great marketing opportunity by giving out eleven principles to respect while designing a training program. Had I chosen to give you 10 I could have called the list "The Ten Commandments of Training" and if I had set my mind on 12 I could have used some reference of donuts or the apostles (being able to put "donuts" and "apostles" in the same sentence is quite a feat in itself). But no, I had to settle for 11. Well, I've never been any at marketing anyways.

In the upcoming chapters I will describe the 11 guidelines to respect when designing your training program. Understand that all of these principles are geared towards one objective: to **maximize the recruitment of the high-threshold motor units**. These motor units are the ones with the greatest potential for muscle growth. They also have the highest force and power production, making them very important for most individuals training for strength, size or speed.

Sadly we are somewhat limited in the number of high-threshold motor units by our genetic makeup. YES it is possible to "convert" some muscle fibers from one type to another and somewhat bypass genetics. However this cannot be accomplished overnight and not to a significant extent either. However by utilizing training methods focusing on the high-threshold motor units, we can selectively develop them; so while their number won't increase, their volume relative to the total muscle volume will increase (so they will comprise most of the muscle without increasing in number). Not to mention that training in a "fast-twitch way" will cause adaptations to all muscle fibers towards a "fast/high-threshold" profile. That means that even though the slow-twitch fibers will not become fast-twitch, their properties and characteristics while lean more towards the "fast" profile. Over time these kind of adaptation will drastically enhance your capacity to gain size, strength and speed.

With that having been said, here are the eleven principles of High-threshold muscle building:

1. Always try to generate as much force as possible
2. Take advantage of the eccentric portion of the movement
3. Precede the maximum concentric action by a prestretch of the muscle
4. Train to the muscle failure point
5. Include some plyometric work to train the nervous system
6. Include a significant amount of unilateral work
7. Include some unstable training to wake-up the nervous system
8. Optimize the work-to-rest ratio
9. Select the most effective exercises for each muscle group
10. When trying to lose fat, add high-speed metabolic work
11. Utilize eccentric loading and deceleration training for strength, power and size

PRINCIPLE 1
Always try to generate as much force as possible

Introduction to the first principle

As we saw earlier, the key to stimulating maximum muscle growth is to not only recruit, but also to fatigue the high-threshold motor units (HTMU). HTMU are also known as type II motor units, fast motor units and glycolitic muscle fibers. There are several different terminologies to describe the different types of motor units/muscle fibers, so weeding through the literature can get confusing. Without going into the depths of theoretical physiology, It is important to have a better understanding of what exactly motor units are and how they are recruited. When we understand how to stimulate these fibers we will be better equipped to design optimal growth training protocols.

The motor unit

The motor unit (MU) is the basic functional unit of the muscle. MU are composed of a set of alpha motor nerves and all the muscle fibers it innervates. All fibers within the same motor unit are of the same sub-type (we will see them more in depth later on). The motor nerve originates at the spinal cord and runs through the muscle where it is "responsible" for the activation of a certain number of muscle fibers. The larger a MU is (composed of more muscle fibers) the more force it can produce. When the nervous system sends an activation signal towards the motor unit, all the fibers innervated by the motor nerve will be recruited maximally; this is the all-or-none principle: basically all the muscle fibers innervated by a same motor nerve will be activated once the signal is sent.

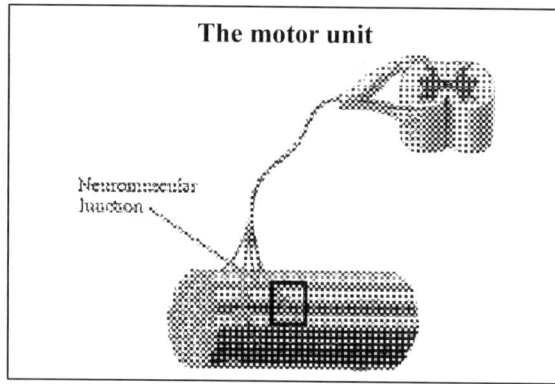 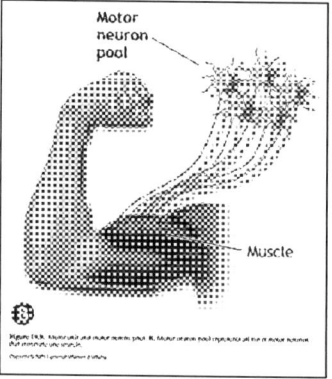

The nature of a MU depends on the type of muscle fibers it is composed of. The original classification system divided muscle fibers into two broad types: Type I (slow) and Type

II (fast). However that classification system has changed due to the discovery of several subtypes of muscle fibers. We have three types of "pure" muscle fibers: I (slow oxidative), IIA (fast oxidative and glycolitic) and IIB (fast glycolitic). There are also several subtypes of these pure fibers as shown with more precision in the following table:

Classification of the human muscle fiber types				
mATPase classification	Speed type	Myosin heavy chain classification	Bioenergetic classification	Fatigue properties
I	Slow	MHCI	Oxidative	Resistant
IC	Slow	MHCI and MHCIIa	Oxidative	Resistant
IIC	Fast	MHCI and MHCIIa	Oxidative-glycolitic	Resistant
IIAC	Fast	MHCIIa and MHCI	Oxidative-glycolitic	Resistant
IIA	Fast	MHCIIa	Oxidative-glycolitic	Resistant
IIAB	Fast	MHCIIa and MHCIIx	Glycolitic	Non-resistant
IIB	Fast	MHCIIx	Glycolitic	Non-resistant

The table presents the muscle fibers in order of force production capacity with the pure I fibers being the least and the pure IIB being the most forceful. Fibers I and IC are part of low-threshold MU, fibers IIC and IIAC are intermediate threshold MU, and fibers IIA, IIAB and IIB are part of high-threshold MU.

Force generation

Your nervous system is responsible for modulating the amount of force produced by your muscles. It does so via:

1. **The number of motor units recruited**: The more motor units are brought into play, the more force you can generate. More force = more motor units (this is a key principle). Under most circumstances, muscle recruitment follows the size principle: the smaller motor units (low threshold) as the demand for force production increases intermediate MU will come into play and if the demand for force production is extremely high, the larger (high-threshold) MU will be recruited. So it should be clear that to recruit the high-threshold motor units, the demand for force production must be very high and to accomplish this it is primordial for each repetition, you make a concentrated maximal voluntary effort.

2. **The firing rate of the recruited motor units**: We just saw that the nervous system can increase force production by recruiting more motor units. Force production can also be modified by varying the rate at which muscle fibers are fired. The more frequently a fiber twitches the more force it can generate. When a muscle fiber twitches at around 50-60 impulses per second, it reaches a titanic contraction which can be up to 10-15 times more forceful than an low firing frequency.

3. **The rate of force development**: When a desired movement requires force to be developed at a very rapid rate, the nervous system can adjust its mode of recruitment by having the motor-units fire at a very high rate. Training that utilize explosive or ballistic concentric actions (or having the intent to accelerate as much as possible) can increase the capacity of the nervous system to utilize muscle fibers at a very high firing rate. We will address this specific point in more depth in the "principle 3" chapter.

The coordination factor: To be efficient at producing force in a movement, your nervous system must be good at coordinating the action of the various motor units within a target muscle. It must also coordinate the action of all the muscles involved in the movement. For that reason, the greatest strength gains from weight training exercises are seen in the movement patterns being trained, with some carryover to other related movements.

Maximum force for maximum stimulation

To recruit the greatest amount of motor units possible, you must generate as much force as possible at any given moment of a set. Some people will be quick to mention that since force production is the key to motor unit recruitment, that we should always lift maximal weights (in the 90-100% range). This is not the case and it shows a lack of understanding of the definition of force. In biomechanics (and physics) force is defined at:

$$\text{"F = ma"}$$

Force (F) equals mass (m) times acceleration (a). So an increase in the generation of force can be accomplished either by increasing the acceleration with a certain load, or by using more weight. Maximum recruitment is generated when the intended force production is its greatest. For that reason, we should try to reach maximum acceleration with any given weight and any given fatigue level. Obviously when the weight used is very heavy, or when we are tired at the end of a set, the actual movement of the bar to be lifted will be slow. However the actual <u>intent to accelerate</u> as much as possible has the same training effect on the nervous system (including MU recruitment, high firing rate, and rapid rate of force development) as if the bar was actually moving fast.

This is what led to the compensatory acceleration technique (CAT). CAT means that you compensate for a non-maximal weight by accelerating it as much as you can; a non-maximal weight lifted without the intent to create as much acceleration as possible will not lead to the recruitment of the high threshold motor units until you reach a level of fatigue that requires your nervous system to finally tap into these strong fibers. So if you were using a moderate load, lifted without CAT you would only have the last 2-3 reps of a set that would actually recruit the HTMUs. And according to Dr. Vladimir Zatsiorsky, a motor unit that is not fatigued is not being trained. As a result, if you are not able to thoroughly fatigue those HTMUs with the last 2-3 reps of a set (if muscle failure occurs due to an accumulation of metabolites for example) that set was wasted, at least when it pertains to stimulating maximal muscle growth.

The fact that you can eventually tap into your HTMU pool as fatigue sets in has led to the saying, "those last few reps are the key" (the most effective for growth). While with regular bodybuilding training this is probably true, using CAT will make each single repetition effective at recruiting the HTMUs. So the HTMUs will get stimulated with 8-12 reps per set, instead of only 2-3. As a result, they are more likely to fatigue, and stimulate to growth.

Key points

1. High-threshold motor units have the greatest growth potential.

2. HTMUs are brought into play when the demand for force production is high.

3. HTMUs can also be brought into play when the fatigue in the intermediate threshold fibers leads to an insufficient force production. Then the HTMUs must be recruited.

4. You can "compensate" for the lack of fatigue in the first reps of a set by always trying to create as much acceleration as possible on each rep of every set.

5. The intent to (trying to) accelerate is responsible for the recruitment of the HTMUs. Even if the bar doesn't move rapidly, if you are really trying to push it as hard as you can, it will have the same effect as actually lifting with great speed.

6. The key is to reach maximum acceleration at a given weight and fatigue level.

PRINCIPLE 2
Take advantage of the eccentric portion of a movement

Introduction to the second principle

The eccentric action of a muscle refers to a resisted lengthening of that muscle; a muscle exerting force while it's being lengthened. This type of action is also called the *yielding* or negative action (as opposed to the *overcoming* action which refers to the actual lifting of the resistance).

Eccentric action is present in most free-weight and machine exercises. However, since concentric strength potential is lower than the eccentric strength potential the yielding portion of a movement is rarely fully stimulated. In other words, the relative weakness of the overcoming portion prevents a complete overload during the yielding portion of the exercise.

As I will explain, it is the yielding portion of an exercise which gives us the greatest bang for our buck. So an individual seeking maximum result should plan training methods emphasizing eccentric overload.

Eccentric stress as a superior stimulus for strength improvements

It's been a while since we've known that the yielding (eccentric/negative) portion of an exercise is responsible for more strength gains than the overcoming (concentric/miometric/positive) portion. For example, a study by Hortobagyi and coworkers found that the total maximal strength improvement from eccentric-only training brought more strength gains than a concentric-only program followed for 6 weeks. Total maximal strength is the sum of maximum concentric, isometric, and eccentric strength. In that parameter, eccentric training gave a mean improvement of 85%, while concentric training led to an improvement of 78%. Furthermore, this study used submaximal yielding actions and maximal overcoming actions. Surely this tells us a lot about the potential of yielding strength training, at least when maximum strength gains are the concern. These results are in accordance with the body of scientific literature on the subject. For example, a study by Higbie et al. (1996) found a combined strength increase (concentric strength improvement + eccentric strength improvement) of 43% with an eccentric-only regimen compared to one of 31.2% with a concentric only regimen. We should also note a study by Hilliard-Robertson and coworkers which concluded that *"A resistance training protocol which includes eccentric as well as concentric exercise, <u>particularly when the eccentric is emphasized</u>, appears to result in greater strength gains than concentric exercise alone"*. This is in accordance with an early study by Komi and Buskirk (1972) which recorded greater strength increases after an eccentric training regimen than after a concentric-only regimen.

It was also found that omitting eccentric stress in a training program severely compromises the potential strength gains (Dudley et al. 1991).

Eccentric stress as a superior stimulus for muscle growth
The last above-mentioned study (Higbie et al. 1996) found that eccentric-only training led to an average muscle size gain of 6.6% over 10 weeks while a concentric-only program led to gains of 5%. While the difference may not seem dramatic, any knowledgeable bodybuilder understands that 2% more muscle over a 10 week period can be visually significant, especially in the long run.

- (Farthing and Chilibeck 2003), which concluded that "eccentric training resulted in greater hypertrophy than concentric training."

- (LaStayo et al. 2003) even found accentuated eccentric training to cause 19% more muscle growth than traditional strength training over 11 weeks!

- *"eccentric muscle actions are a necessary stimulus for muscle hypertrophy"* (Cote et al. 1988).

Why is eccentric training effective?

Eccentric training allows one to stimulate greater strength and size gains than pure concentric training. There are five major reasons why:

1. There is a greater neural adaptation to eccentric training than to concentric training (Hortobagyi et al. 1996).

2. There is a more important force output produced during a maximal eccentric action (greater overload) because you can use a higher external load (Colliander and Tesch 1990).

3. There is a higher level of stress per motor unit during eccentric work. Less motor units are recruited during the eccentric portion of a movement, thus each of the recruited motor units receives much more stimulation (Grabiner and Owings 2002, Linnamo et al. 2002). Furthermore, since the nervous systems seems to recruit less motor units during a maximal eccentric action, the potential for improvement could be greater than with maximal concentric action.

4. There is some evidence that maximal eccentric actions will preferably recruit fast-twitch muscle fibers (high threshold motor units), which are more responsive to muscle growth and strengthening (Nardone et al. 1989, Howell et al. 1995, Hortobagyi et al. 1996). In fact, eccentric training may stimulate an evolution towards a faster contractile profile (Martin et al. 1995).

5. Most of the micro-trauma to the muscle cells incurred during training is a result of the eccentric action (Brown et al. 1997, Gibala et al. 2000). It has been established that this micro-trauma acts as the signal to start the muscle adaptation process (Clarke and Feedback, 1996).

Key points

1. If you de-emphasize the yielding portion of your strength exercises (lowering the bar very fast, not contracting your muscles during the eccentric portion, etc.) you might as well not be training at all (at least if maximum strength and size are important to you). Be careful though, it doesn't mean that you should accentuate/emphasize the eccentric stress in all of your exercises, just that some exercises should target a very large eccentric overload.

2. Accentuating the eccentric stress during a session will lead to more strength gains. The reasons are related to structural as well as neural adaptations.

3. The eccentric portion of a movement is the main stimulus for muscle growth as it is the cause of most of the micro-trauma inflicted on the muscles, which acts as the signal to kick the muscle building process into overdrive.

4. One more benefit that I have found from experience is that overloading the eccentric portion of an exercise allows one to get used to holding big weights and controlling them. This can have a very important confidence-building effect when attempting to lift maximum weights.

How to take advantage of the eccentric portion of an exercise

The first way to take advantage of the eccentric portion of an exercise is to adjust the way you perform that phase of the movement for each repetition of every set of every one of your "normal" training exercises. The second approach is to use eccentric-only training as a special training technique, but this will be discussed more in depth in the chapter detailing the ninth principle.

The current trend in bodybuilding/muscle gain training is to execute the eccentric portion of an exercise slowly or at least under control (lowering the weight in 3-4 seconds).

While this is already far superior to bouncing the weight up and down it is not 100% optimal to maximize muscle growth; or at least it is somewhat incomplete.

Why is it incomplete? It is possible to lower a weight under control by relying on intramuscular and intermuscular friction as well as relying on the non-targeted muscle groups: the target muscles can actually relax even though you are controlling the weight as you are lowering it. Most powerlifters use the coaching queue "lower the bar with your lats when you bench press": by flaring out your lats, the friction between your inner arm and your lats will breakdown the descent, allowing the chest, triceps and deltoid muscles to work to a lesser extent (conserving energy for the actual lifting portion). This is good if you want to max out on a lift. However, to simulate maximal muscle growth it isn't optimal. Maximum hypertrophy stimulation is achieved if there are no breaks in muscle tension during a set. This means that the target muscles should always contract maximally during the whole movement (thus you should not rely on friction during the eccentric portion of the exercise) and also that you should never pause between reps during a set. Keep those muscles under tension!

Not only should you lower the weight under control, you should be flexing the target muscle group as hard as you can during that portion of the exercise. To accomplish this you must focus on the feeling of the muscle contraction (internal training) rather than on the actual lifting of the bar (external training). As I always say, when you are lifting to build muscle mass you do not lift weights, you contract muscles against a resistance.

That's how the first ¾ of the eccentric phase should be performed: slow with a maximal muscular contraction/tension. Doing this will already make each and every repetition drastically more effective than simply "lowering the weight under control". But to make it a "perfect eccentric rep" we need to add a second phase which occurs during the last ¼ of the eccentric portion of a repetition.

Studies have shown that a rapid eccentric action occurring when a muscle is stretched can drastically increase high-threshold motor unit recruitment. It can also potentiate the subsequent concentric movement. This is the principle behind the various plyometric training exercises used by athletes. When a muscle is forcefully and rapidly stretched under load you can increase the amount of force you can produce in the actual lifting phase (this is due to the activation of the myotatic stretch reflex, to the elastic components of the muscle tissue as well as to an increased recruitment of high-threshold motor units). This method can be applied to regular lifting exercise and is a very powerful growth producing method.

To do this you execute the first ¾ of the eccentric phase slowly under max tension (to reap the hypertrophy-stimulating benefits) and as you get close to the end of the eccentric range of motion, accelerate the weight downward to stretch it forcefully under load. As you reach the fully stretched position you explode upwards using the compensatory acceleration principle. The exact way of performing this technique safely will be discussed in the next chapter. But for now remember that the perfect eccentric rep starts with a slow, flexed phase and ends with a rapid stretch phase.

Key points

1. The first ¾ of the eccentric phase should not only be performed slowly and under control, but also while the target muscle group is being tensed to its maximum.

2. In the last ¼ of the eccentric phase you should increase the speed of movement until you reach the fully stretched position to maximize force production and HTMU recruitment.

PRINCIPLE 3
Precede the maximum concentric action by a prestretch of the muscle

Introduction

The advantages of performing a high velocity prestretch before an explosive concentric action is well known in the world of sports. This type of movement, known as the stretch-shorten cycle (SSC) is the natural way our muscles work in most tasks requiring a high force production of a ballistic nature (throwing, jumping, etc.) as well as in locomotion tasks (walking, running, hopping, etc.). In muscle contractions preceding the concentric phase (the lifting portion in our case) by a short and forceful stretch can significantly increase the amount of force produced. This is due to:

1. **The potentiating effect of the myotatic stretch-reflex**: When a musculotendinous structure (a muscle and its tendons) is forcefully stretched, there is the onset of a "stretch reflex" governed by the activation of the muscle spindles. Muscle spindles are small fibers that run parallel to your muscle fibers and when they are stretched beyond a certain point they initiate the myotatic stretch reflex that helps the body to shorten. This is a protective mechanism designed to protect the musculotendinous structures against tears caused by excessive stretching.

2. **The elastic component of the musculotendinous structure**: The muscles, fascias and tendons are elastic by nature (more or less depending on the structure) and just like a rubber band; if they are stretched they will tend to shorten powerfully in return. This characteristic of the musculotendinous structures can also contribute to an increase in force production.

3. **The increase in motor-units activation**: Walshe et al. (1998) have stated that prestretching a muscle prior to a concentric phase promotes a higher active muscle state. They also found that stretch-induced movements the forceful stretch could potentiate the capacity of the contractile elements of the muscle.

4. **The evolution toward a fast-twitch muscle fiber dominance over the long run**: Paddon-Jones et al. (2001) have demonstrated that rapid eccentric actions (the forceful and rapid stretch at the end of the eccentric phase represent a rapid eccentric action) lead

to an increase in fast-twitch fibers/motor-units over the long run (using a 10 week protocol in the study). Fast eccentric movements decreased type I fibers from an average of 53.8% to an average of 39.1% while type IIb fiber percentage increased from an average of 5.8% to an average of 12.9% (thus, there must have been a significant increase in IIa fibers too, but was not measured). In the long term, this type of training effect could greatly improve an individual's capacity to stimulate hypertrophy as well as strength and power gains.

To be effective, a stretch-shorten cycle require three essential conditions (Komi and Gollhofer, 1997):

a) **A short and rapid eccentric phase**: This short eccentric/prestretch phase (the prestretch phase is only the last ¼ of the eccentric phase for us and the technique I recommend) favors the utilisation of short-range elastic stiffness and lead to a greater force production.

b) **A short coupling-time**: The coupling-time refers to the transition between the prestretch and the following concentric action. It has been shown that the shorter the coupling-time (very rapid change from stretch to contract) is associated with a much higher increase in force production.

c) **A well-timed preactivation of the muscles prior to the rapid prestretch**: This is what we accomplish by performing the initial ¾ of the eccentric phase under control and maximal muscle tension; contracting the muscles hard during that portion of the movement will ensure that the muscles are properly activated before the stretch. A powerful stretch without an adequate preactivation can be dangerous and vastly decrease the efficiency of the prestretch.

On a similar note, it is interesting that excessive kinetic energy accumulation prior to the stretch can actually lead to a decrease in force production, as opposed to an increase. This is due to the activation of the protective mechanisms of the muscles (particularly the

Golgi tendon organs). This explains, in part, why only the last ¼ of the eccentric phase should be done rapidly. The initial ¾ should be controlled to avoid excessive kinetic energy build-up.

Not only can a prestretch enhance force production, but it can also increase force production at any given training velocity. Normally muscle contractions respond to the inverse force-velocity curve proposed by Hill (illustrated below).

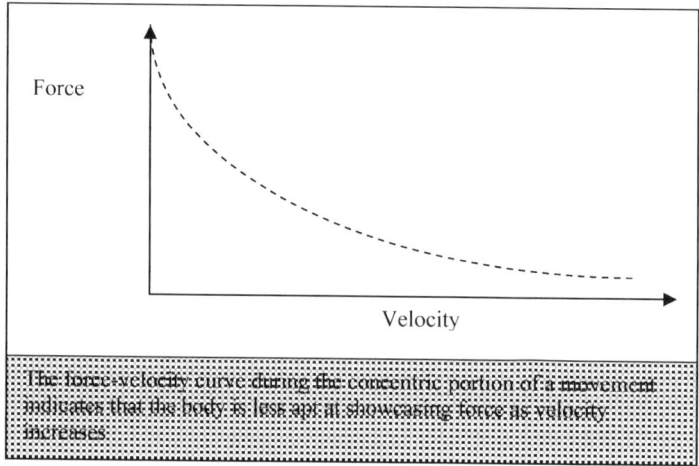

The force-velocity curve during the concentric portion of a movement indicates that the body is less apt at showcasing force as velocity increases.

However, this curve was developed from non-SSC movements. The force-velocity curve during movements involving the SSC is different. The following graphic adapted from Komi et al. (1996) illustrates the difference between the theoretical force-velocity curve, and the one observed with SSC movements.

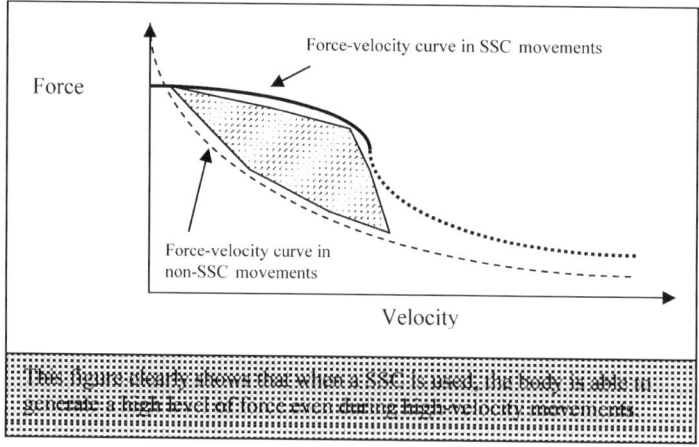

This figure clearly shows that when a SSC is used, the body is able to generate a high level of force even during high-velocity movements.

Key points

1. A short and rapid prestretch enhances force production via reflex, elastic and contraction factors.

2. Long-term use of this training technique can increase the ratio of fast-twitch muscle fibers and decrease the ratio of slow-twitch ones. This will vastly increase your muscle growth potential.

3. To be effective, a prestretch must be short and rapid, preceded by an adequate muscle preactivation, and performed with a minimal coupling-time between the stretch and the following contraction.

4. The prestretch increases the body's capacity to sustain a high level of force production, even at high velocity of movement.

The controlled muscle preactivation phase

This refers to the first ¾ of the eccentric phase of the movement. As we saw in the preceding chapter, this phase should be performed under control while the muscles are maximally tensed. This will increase the safety and efficacy of the prestretch phase. The biggest mistake you could make during that initial phase would be to lower the weight too fast without the muscles being adequately tensed. This will make the technique dangerous (no one builds muscles when in the hospital) and less effective. Particular attention to the movement pattern should be emphasised: you should use the movement pattern that will allow you to "feel" the target muscle working optimally. This aspect will be discussed in the exercise selection section.

The prestretch phase

The way to perform this phase of the movement should be pretty obvious by now: the last ¼ of the eccentric phase should be performed rapidly to allow for a forceful prestretch of the targeted muscle. It is also very important to initiate the subsequent lifting phase as fast as possible after the prestretch has occurred to reap the most benefits from this technique.

VERY important point

> You will notice that I mentioned that the prestretch should be done more rapidly than the initial eccentric portion which is slow. However, this doesn't mean that you should be jerking down or bouncing the weight uncontrollably! You still must maintain proper muscle tension and keep the bar under full control to avoid any potential injury.

The maximum acceleration lifting phase

As we saw in the first chapter (principle 1) to generate the maximum force possible with a given weight, you must try to generate as much acceleration as possible during the lifting/concentric phase. This is even more important when using a prestretch because the biggest advantage of this prestretch is that it increases your capacity to produce more force (remember that force = mass x acceleration) during high-speed movements. When you try to accelerate as much as possible (as we saw earlier, the intent to accelerate is as important as the actual movement speed) you increase the recruitment of the high-threshold motor-units and you upregulate their firing frequency. As a result, you use more of the "money fibers" and you make them work harder.

Key points

1. Start with a controlled and tensed eccentric movement during the first ¾ of the phase. This creates a proper muscle preactivation state and will allow you to better focus on the target muscle.

2. End the eccentric portion by a rapid and forceful stretch to increase the force production during the subsequent lifting action.

3. As soon as you reach the prestretch position, initiate the lifting action as fast as you can. Remember to try to generate as much acceleration as you can on each rep. As fatigue sets in, the actual speed of the reps will decrease, but the intent to accelerate has the same training effect as the actual speed of the movement.

PRINCIPLE 4
Training to the positive muscle failure point

Introduction

Few concepts in the world of strength training have been more hotly debated than the need (or not) to reach muscle failure during your sets. Is it necessary for muscle growth? No. However, I feel it is necessary for optimal growth. Some argue that training to failure is either dangerous or can lead to CNS fatigue. Others argue that training to failure too often will cause too much muscle damage and can lead to localised overtraining. Some of these misconceptions stem from the fact that muscle failure is not well understood.

The biggest proponents of training to failure have defined it as "creating a maximum amount of inroads to the muscle on each set". <u>This is fine and well however am I the only one who doesn't understand what they mean by that?</u> It is important to correctly describe what muscle failure is and why it happens. This information will allow us to make an objective assessment of the need (or not) of training to failure.

What is the point of failure?

Failure is easy to understand. It's simply the incapacity to maintain the required amount of force output (Edwards 1981, Davis 1996). In other words, at some point during your set, completing more repetitions will become more and more arduous until you are unable to produce the required amount of force to complete a repetition. Failure isn't the amount of "inroad" to the muscle; it's nothing esoteric as we just saw.

The causes of failure

If the concept of training to failure is actually quite easy to grasp, the causes underlying this occurrence are a bit more complex. There is no exclusive cause of training failure; rather there are quite a few of them.

1. **Central/Neuromuscular factors**: the nervous system is the boss! It's the CNS that recruits the motor-units involved in the movement, set their firing rate and ensure proper intra and intermuscular coordination. Central fatigue can contribute to muscle failure, especially the depletion of the neurotransmitters dopamine and acetylcholine. A decrease in acetylcholine levels is associated with a decrease in the efficiency of the

neuromuscular transmission. In other words, when acetylcholine levels are low, it's harder for your CNS to recruit motor-units.

2. **Psychological factors**: The perception of exhaustion or exercise discomfort can lead to a premature ending of a set. This is especially true of beginners who are not accustomed to the pain of training intensely. Subconsciously (or not) the individual will decrease his force production as the set becomes uncomfortable. This is obviously not an "acceptable" cause of failure in the intermediate or advanced trainees, but beginners who are not used to intense training could slowly break into it by gradually increasing their pain tolerance.

3. **Metabolic and mechanical factors**: It is well known that an increase in blood acidity reduces the magnitude of the neural drive as well as the whole neuromuscular process. Lactic acid and lactate are sometimes thought to be the cause of this acidification of the blood, but this is actually not the case. The real culprit is hydrogen. Hydrogen ions can increase blood acidity, inhibits the PFK enzyme (reducing the capacity to produce energy from glucose), interferes with the formation of the actin-myosin cross bridges (necessary for muscle contraction to occur) and decrease the sensitivity of the troponin to calcium ions. Potassium ions can also play a role in muscle fatigue during a set. Sejersted (2000) has demonstrated that intense physical activity markedly increases extra-cellular levels of potassium ions. Potassium accumulation outside the muscle cell leads to a dramatic loss of force which obviously makes muscle action more difficult. Finally we can include phosphate molecules into the equation. Phosphate is a by-product of the breadown of ATP to produce energy. An accumulation of phosphate decreases the sensitivity of the sarcoplasmic reticulum to calcium ions. Without going into excessive detail, this desensitization reduces the capacity to produce a decent muscle contraction.

4. **Energetic factors**: Muscle contraction requires energy. Strength training relies first and foremost on the use of glucose/glucogen for fuel with the phophagen system (ATP-CP) also playing a role. Intramuscular glycogen levels (glucose reserve in the muscle) is very limited and can become depleted as the training session progresses. The body can compensate by mobilizing glucose stored elsewhere in the body (but this amount is also

finite), by transforming amino acids into glucose (which is a less powerful way of producing energy for intense muscle contractions), or turn to free fatty acids and ketone bodies. The last two solutions cannot provide energy as fast as intramuscular glycogen can. As a result, even though it will be possible to continue exercising with a depleted muscle, it is impossible to maintain the same level of intensity and force production.

So as you can see, it is impossible to attribute muscle failure to a single phenomenon. Rather, it's a mix of several factors that cause muscle failure. Contrary to popular beliefs, reaching muscle failure in one set doesn't ensure the complete fatigue and stimulation of all the muscle fibers in a muscle. Far from it! Failure can occur way before full contractile fatigue has been reached. This means that the "one set per exercise to failure" method is not ideal for maximal growth. As a part of a more complex training system it can be beneficial from time to time, but not as a discrete training system.

At some point it becomes necessary to increase training volume to fully stimulate a larger pool of muscle fibers. Remember that simply recruiting a motor-unit doesn't mean that it's been stimulated. To be stimulated a muscle fiber must be recruited and fatigued (Zatsiorsky 1996).

If training to failure doesn't ensure full motor-unit stimulation within a muscle, not taking a set to positive muscle failure (the point where a technically correct full repetition cannot be completed) is even less effective since it will not fatigue the HTMUs as much and remember that a muscle fiber that isn't fatigued isn't fully stimulated! In other words training to failure doesn't guarantee maximal motor-unit stimulation but not taking a set to failure drastically reduces the efficacy of a set. This indicates that high volume of work without going to failure isn't ideal for maximal muscle growth (but it's okay for strength and power oriented training). But the other end of the spectrum: low-volume training taken to failure isn't ideal either. Failure and volume are both needed for maximal motor-unit stimulation. That's not to say that you should use a huge volume of work, but a moderate volume of sets taken to failure is necessary for maximal muscle growth.

And what about the so-called CNS drain that can occur when you take your sets to failure? While I do agree that for continuous improvements to occur one should avoid CNS burnout/overtraining (also called the Central Fatigue Syndrome). I understand the theory behind avoiding going to failure: going to failure increases the implication of the nervous system because as fatigue sets in (accumulation of metabolites and energetic depletion) it must work harder to recruit the last HTMUs. The argument is that we should minimize training that has a high demand on the nervous system. However, most people who espouse the "don't go to failure" theory are generally proponents of heavy lifting and/or explosive lifting. Both of which are just as demanding (if not more) on the nervous system as training to failure.

Why are they against one neural intensive method but for another one? The fact is that the nervous system is an adaptive system just like the rest of our body and it can become more efficient at stimulating muscle contraction when it's trained properly. And while the CFS is a real problem, its occurrence in bodybuilders or individual training for muscle mass gains is minimal, close to nil. Sure, we can suffer from CNS fatigue after a training session (just like our muscles are fatigued too), but the body can recover from that. Neurotransmitter depletion might be a concern, but rarely is a real problem. Using a supplement like Biotest's Power Drive can help in that regard by boosting acetylcholine and dopamine levels.

Key points

1, Muscle failure isn't an indication that every muscle fiber within a muscle has been fully stimulated.

2. Muscle failure can occur because of neural, psychological, metabolic or energetic factors.

3. A moderate amount of work to failure is required for full motor-unit stimulation within a muscle.

PRINCIPLE 5
Including some plyometric work to train the nervous system

Introduction

Plyometric training, also known as shock training, was developed by Yuri Verkhoshansky in 1977. The objective of this method is to increase concentric power and force output by stimulating the muscles and reflexes via "shock stretching" action preceding the overcoming portion of the movement. This is accomplished by dropping from a certain height (typically 0.4m to 0.7m, although heights of up to 1.1m have been used by very advanced athletes) to elicit a powerful stretch activation, then jumping up as high as possible immediately upon landing.

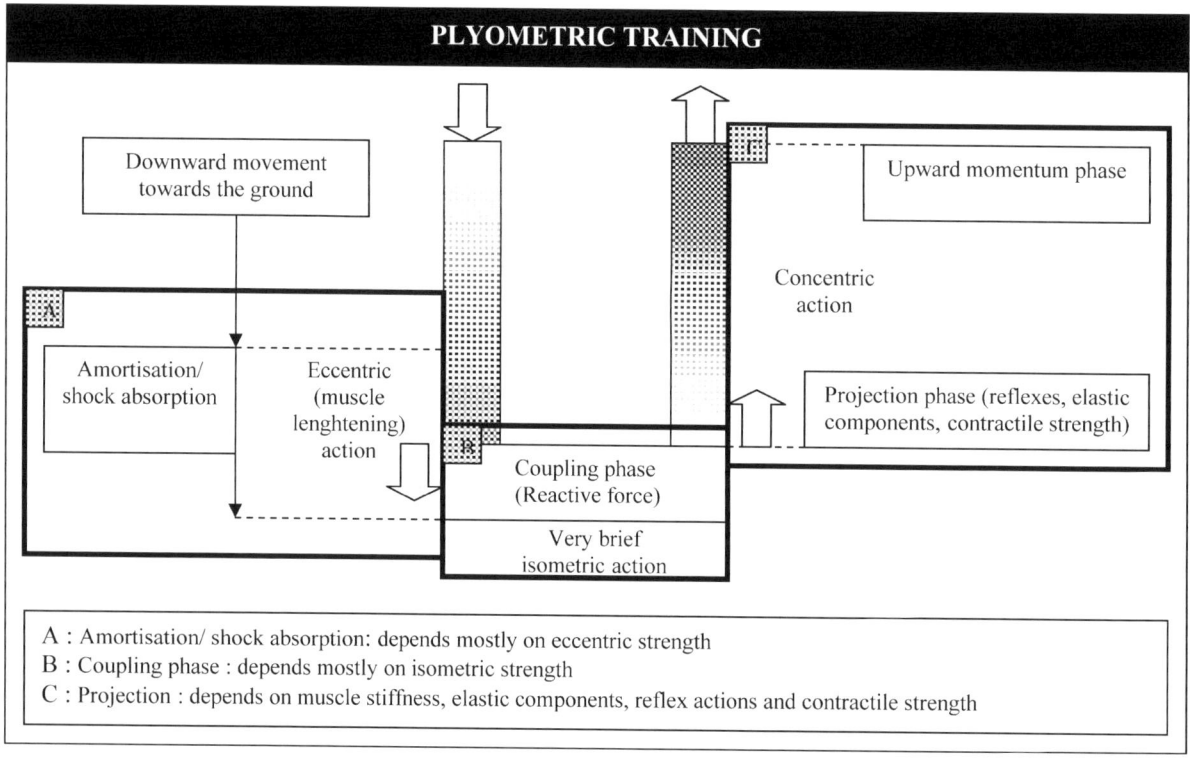

It has been well established in both Eastern and Western studies that plyometric, or shock training, can significantly increase power production during explosive concentric movements. This is mostly due to the following factors:

1. **An increase in reactive strength**: Reactive strength refers to the capacity to rapidly switch from an eccentric/yielding action to a concentric/overcoming action. Lack of

reactive strength will lead to a longer coupling time and, consequently, lower force and power production during the overcoming portion of the movement (Kurz 2001).

2. **Neural adaptations :** Viitasalo et al. (1998) found a different neural response between athletes doing a lot of jumping and untrained individuals when doing a depth jump. Jumpers were able to activate more motor units during the movement (greater EMG) and plan the motor command faster (higher and more rapid pre-action EMG). Kyröläinen et al. (1991) also found that 16 weeks of depth jump training led to better jumping efficiency. Schmidtbleicher (1987 and 1982) found that trained subjects were able to use the kinetic energy produced during the eccentric portion of a depth jump, while in untrained subjects this eccentric period was actually inhibiting instead of potentiating! Finally, Walshe et al. (1998) concluded that the superiority of depth jump training over regular jump training was due to *"the attainment of a higher active muscle state,"* meaning that the fast eccentric portion of the movement increased muscle activation.

3. **Structural adaptations:** Shock training has been reported to cause some muscle soreness and muscle damage (Horita et al. 1999). This is understandable since the eccentric force produced is very high, albeit rapid. This may indicate that plyometrics are a powerful stimulus to stimulate structural adaptations. However, depth jumps do not lead to significant hypertrophy. So the nature of the structural adaptations following depth jumping is not quantitative in nature, but qualitative: an improvement of the strength and contractile capacity of each muscle fiber.

Plyometric training actually responds to the same "rules" that commands the effectiveness of using a rapid muscle prestretch prior to a concentric/lifting action. For that reason everything mentioned in the chapter on principle 3 will apply to plyometric training.

For those of us who are mostly interested in gaining muscle mass, the main benefit of plyometric work is to improve the CNS' capacity to recruit HTMUs as fast as possible during the initial part of a lifting movement and to train our motor units to fire at a high rate.

Types of plyometric work

There are two main types of plyometric work: low-intensity and high-intensity plyo work. The high-intensity plyometrics do have a more profound effect on the nervous system, but they can also be more stressful to the joints, tendons, and ligaments. As such, they have a very powerful effect but cannot be used for more than 4 weeks at a time. Low-intensity plyo work isn't as stressful on the CNS and won't be detrimental to joint health; as such it can be used much more frequently than the high-intensity version. While the training effect won't be as pronounced, you will still activate the HTMUs and use a high firing rate.

High-intensity plyometric work

This is the form of plyometric training that is known as shock training. It refers to the depth jump (and its variations) and the depth push-up (and its variations). The basic principle is to stand on an elevated surface and then let yourself fall off. Immediately as your feet (or ands) touch the floor, you rebound upwards by jumping (propelling) yourself as high as possible.

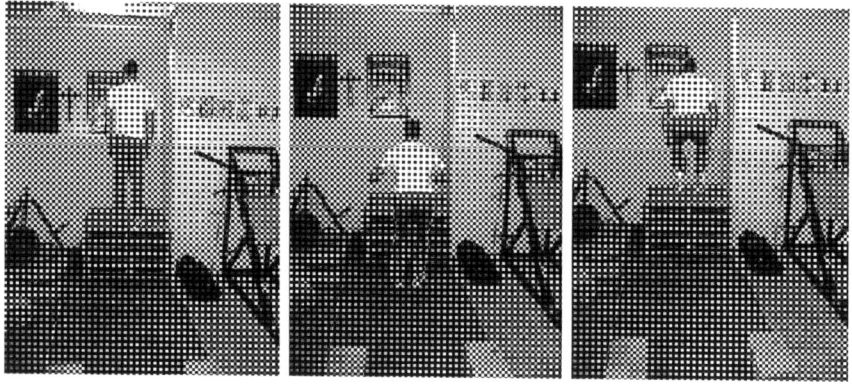

Soviet literature gives the following guidelines when practicing depth jumps:

1. The joint position upon landing should be as close as possible to that of an important sport action (Laputin and Oleshko 1982).

2. The amortization phase should be short enough to avoid losing the elastic energy produced, but long enough to allow for the shock stretching to occur (Laputin and Oleshko 1982). Research indicates that the elastic energy from landing is stored for up to 2 seconds. So, in theory you have a window of 2 seconds between the landing and take-off phase. However, to maximize the training effect you should not spend more than 1 second on the floor.

3. The height of the drop should be regulated by the preparedness of the athlete. The heels should not touch the ground during the landing phase. If they do, then the height of the drop is too high (Laputin and Oleshko 1982). A height varying from 0.5m to 0.7m appears to be ideal for most strength and power athletes (Roman 1986).

4. Depth jumps have a very powerful training effect, so the volume of work should be low; i.e. no more than 4 sets of 10 repetitions (or 40 total jumps spread over more sets), 2-3 times per week for advanced athletes and 3 sets of 5-8 repetitions (or 15-24 total jumps spread over more sets), and 1-2 times per week for lower classes of athletes (Laputin and Oleshko 1982). The problem with many coaches and athletes is that they don't feel that depth jumping is hard; it's not very tiring compared to other means of training. Because of this, they do too high a volume of depth jumps.

Low-intensity plyometric work
This type of training refers to everything that falls into normal jumping exercises, hopping, bounding, etc. For the upper body we can also include medicine ball throws in that category.

Key points

1. Plyometric work has a training effect on the nervous system, on the muscle reflexes and on the muscles/tendons themselves.

2. For us who are interested primarily in gaining muscle mass, the main advantage of plyometric work is the increase in HTMUs activation it can lead to.

3. Low-intensity plyometric work can be performed for long periods of time while the high-intensity versions should be limited to blocks of 2-4 weeks at a time.

PRINCIPLE 6
Including a significant amount of unilateral work

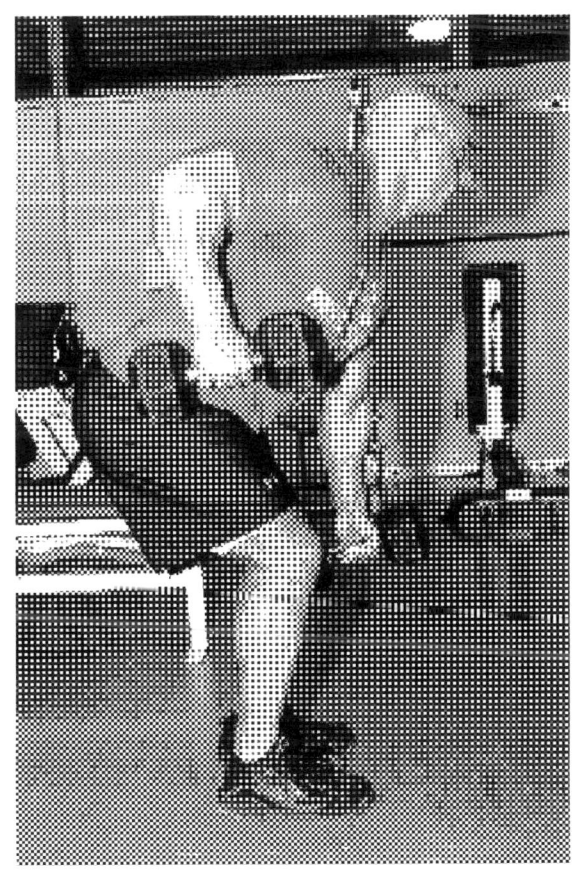

Introduction

In the world of sport science, there is an interesting phenomenon that has often been neglected when it comes to training aimed at building maximum muscle mass. This concept is called the bilateral deficit (BLD) and it refers to the fact that normally you cannot produce as much force when both contralateral limbs are performing the exercise simultaneously as when we exercise each limb individually and add the force of each side. For example, the sum of your maximum leg extension strength with both legs will be inferior to the sum of your right leg extension strength and your left leg extension strength when they are working individually.

For this discussion, understand that bilateral exercises refer to movements where the same limb(s) of both sides work at the same time and do the same task. Any barbell lift is bilateral, dumbbell exercises where both sides work at the same time are also bilateral. Machine and cable work where both sides are involved at the same time are also bilateral. Unilateral exercise refers to movements where each side is worked independently or alternatively (e.g. a lunge, a step-up, 1-leg extension, 1-leg curl, 1-leg press, alternate dumbbell curl, alternate DB shoulder press, etc.).

The importance of the bilateral deficit varies depending on the training level of the athlete: beginners have a greater BLD (they are a lot less efficient in movements with both limbs) while advanced athletes have less of a BLD. Training experience can also play a role since athletes who training mostly on bilateral exercises will not have a BLD that's as important as athletes who rarely use bilateral training. Limb length also plays a role in the phenomenon: individuals with longer limbs normally have a greater bilateral deficit. Finally, individuals with a very efficient nervous system (effective at recruiting high-threshold motor units) will have less of a bilateral deficit, in some cases athletes with a super efficient CNS and who spend all of their time on bilateral exercises (Olympic lifters and powerlifters for example) can actually have a bilateral facilitation instead of a deficit.

The BLD can be attributed to local neural control mechanisms (Howard & Enoka 1991) and a decreased recruitment of high-threshold motor units (Vandervoort et al. 1984). In other words, individuals with a large BLD will not be able to stimulate as much growth if relying only on bilateral movements because they will have a harder time recruiting their high-threshold motor units.

Key points

1. It's harder for the body to recruit the HTMUs during bilateral than during unilateral exercises. The greater the BLD is, the more pronounced this effect will be.

2. Beginners, athletes with an inefficient CNS, and individuals with long limbs normally have a greater bilateral deficit and as a result they will have a harder time recruiting HTMUs during bilateral work.

3. As an individual becomes better trained and more efficient at recruiting the HTMUs, the bilateral deficit will decrease as their capacity to recruit the HTMUs during bilateral work will increase.

Training applications

It now seems obvious that unilateral work should be part of a good training program. This inclusion is especially important with beginner, long-limbed individuals, and those with an inefficient nervous system. Advanced athletes and those with a very efficient CNS don't need to include as much unilateral work, although it should still remain present in the training program.

We should avoid falling into the extreme though. Unilateral work is very good, but that doesn't mean that you should drop all bilateral work! Training on bilateral exercises decrease the bilateral deficit over time while unilateral training doesn't (Janzen et al. 2006). So if an individual drops all bilateral work from his program, he will never reduce his BLD. Beginners and long-limbed individuals should include more unilateral work to be able to recruit more HTMUs while they also work on correcting their bilateral deficit with bilateral movements.

Key points

1. Beginner and long-limbed individuals should include more unilateral work to fully stimulate their HTMUs while also including bilateral work for every muscle group to correct the bilateral deficit. In other words the beginner wants to correct his bilateral deficit but while he does so, he should include more unilateral work to still be able to stimulate as much growth as possible.

2. As an individual gains more experience, his CNS will become more efficient at recruiting the HTMUs and as a result his bilateral deficit will decrease. They can increase the amount of bilateral and decrease unilateral work (while still keeping it in the program).

PRINCIPLE 7
Including some unstable training to activate the nervous system

Introduction

Another controversial topic when it comes to building muscle is the use of unstable exercises; movements performed where the base of support is unstable would theoretically have the potential to increase muscle activation in an attempt to achieve proper joint and movement stability (Lehman et al. 2006). So in theory, it would seem that unstable training could increase muscle activation due to an increased demand on the neuromuscular system in order to stabilize the articulation joints rendered unstable by the surface used as a base of support. Still in theory that could mean that unstable exercise could improve the capacity of the nervous system to activate certain muscles. Performing a push-up movement with the hands on a swiss ball increases triceps activation significantly compared to a regular push-up (22% activation for stable, 43% for unstable). Changes in pectoral activation were positive with the unstable push-up, but didn't reach statistical significance (21% activation for stable, 26.6% for unstable) this still shows a tendency towards greater activation of the pectorals with this exercise (Lehman et al. 2006). However, when the push ups were performed with the feet on the ball instead of the hands, there was no difference in muscle activation. This would seem to indicate that to increase upper body muscle activation, the unstable surface should be under the hands and not the feet. It would also seem that the closer a muscle is to the source of instability, the more activation potentiation there is while muscles far away from the the source of instability are not affected as much.

However, an argument against the use of unstable movements is that force production during these exercises is lower compared to similar exercises performed on a stable surface (Anderson and Behm, 2001). As we saw earlier, force production is one of the most important factors governing the recruitment of the HTMUs. So it's possible that a technique leading to lesser force production could decrease the efficiency of an exercise.

Unstable training has been widely used for rehabilitation and injury prevention purposes with a considerable amount of success. Naughton et al. (2005) found unstable upper body exercise effective at improving proprioception at the shoulder joint. However, the application of this type of training is not well understood when it comes to mass building purposes. There seems to be two distinct camps in the regard to unstable exercises utilization: those who do almost everything on an unstable surface and those who never use this method. Very few are in the middle and even fewer make a logical utilisation of this technique.

Key points

1. Unstable exercise can increase neuromuscular activation of the muscles due to the need to stabilize the body.

2. Unstable strength exercise (weight lifting performed on an unstable surface) leads to a lesser force production which could hurt HTMUs recruitment.

3. To increase muscle activity the unstable surface should be under the hands for the upper body and under the feet for the lower body (any instability increases core muscles activation).

4. The closer a muscle is to the source of instability, the higher will the increase in activation be.

Correct application of unstable training

I will be clear right away: unstable strength exercise cannot and will not lead to the stimulation of as much muscle growth as stable variations of the movements. The decrease in force production will prevent maximum motor unit recruitment. As a result, using unstable variations of weight lifting exercise makes very little sense.

The main use of unstable training is to increase CNS activity. To "wake-up" the nervous system, so to speak. The nervous system will have to work harder to maintain proper stability during the movement. So when you perform an unstable movement, you better prepare the nervous system to perform optimally during regular lifting exercises: the CNS will be potentiated by the unstable training and this will lead to greater motor unit activation during the subsequent lifting drills.

So, the correct application of unstable exercise when muscle growth is the main concern is as a CNS activator. As such, it should be performed before a stable exercise with the same movement structure or muscle involvement (e.g. push-ups with the hands on a swiss ball before moving on to DB bench press). This can be done either as a superset (one set of unstable exercise, no rest, one set of stable exercise) in alternate fashion (one set of unstable exercise, brief rest period, one set of stable exercise) or as a separate drill within a workout. In the later case, the unstable exercise should be used at the beginning of the workout. However, the best option for maximum muscle growth stimulation seems to be either to superset or alternate both type of exercise.

You don't have to use an unstable exercise for every body part or movement structure, but it can be a good tool to use for a stubborn muscle group. A stubborn muscle is often as such because of a lack of activation from the CNS so using an unstable exercise could help solve that problem.

Also note that to be "unstable" an exercise doesn't necessarily have to be performed on an unstable surface. Simply reducing the base of support (e.g. lunges on your toes, single-leg squat, single leg Romanian deadlift, etc.) can also do the trick.

Key points

> 1. Unstable training should be used to activate the nervous system prior to the real strength training exercises.
>
> 2. You don't have to use an unstable surface to make an exercise unstable: you can simply reduce the base of support, increasing the need for balance.

PRINCIPLE 8
Optimize the work-to-rest ratio

Introduction

While the actual amount and quality of work performed are very important for stimulating maximum muscle growth, the significance of the work-to-rest ratio shouldn't be underestimated either. This ratio plays a huge role when it comes to initiating the adaptation process and will thus have an important effect on the amount of muscle you will add to your frame.

There are several "levels" to the work-to-rest ratio; each of them playing a key role in the training process:

1. **Intraset work-to-rest ratio**
2. **Workout density**
3. **Weekly work-to-restoration ratio**

Intraset work-to-rest ratio

This refers to the time proportion during a set where the muscle is under maximal tension. For example, if a set lasts 40 seconds and the muscles are tensed maximally for 25 of these seconds, the intraset ratio would be 62.5%. In other words, your muscles would be fully tensed 62.5% of the time while during the remaining 37.5% of the time they would either be relaxed or less than maximally tensed either because you are pausing between reps, lowering the weight without maximally contracting your muscle, or lifting the weight without trying to generate as much force as possible. If you are training to gain as much muscle mass as you can, you should strive to have an intraset ratio as close to 100% as possible. This means not taking pauses between reps, always flexing your muscles as hard as possible during the eccentric portion of the movement, and always trying to lift the weight with as much force/acceleration as possible. It also means avoiding unloading the muscles. Unloading occurs when the weight is not supported by the muscles but by the skeletal structure (for example, the arms locked out during a bench press). So, during movements such as pressing exercises, squats, leg presses, and hack squats you should stop just short of lockout to keep the muscles under load.

Workout density

Density refers to the ratio of work per unit of time during a workout. If you are actively training for 30 minutes during a 70 minute workout you have a density of around 43%. In other words, you spend 43% of your training time actively working out and 57% of it resting. When training for muscle mass gains you should strive to increase workout density as much as you can without having to decrease the quality of each set. This means using as little rest as possible between your sets. How much rest should you take? I can't give you an exact number because this will vary depending on the muscle(s) being trained, the exercise selection, and your level of conditioning. But you should shoot for incomplete restoration; don't wait to be fully recovered before starting a new set. First and foremost, you should try to reach an important oxygen debt after each set, an oxygen debt is when you are out of breath after the set. The harder and deeper you have to breathe after a set, the more productive (when it comes to building muscle mass) it was. Obviously you will have a greater oxygen debt after a set of squats than after a set of dumbbell curl, but regardless of the exercise you should strive to attain the greatest oxygen debt possible with that exercise. You will be breathing hard after a set and you shouldn't wait for your breathing to normalize before starting a new set. Incomplete rest is what you want: start a set when you are still breathing somewhat hard. Cumulative fatigue is a very important stimulus for muscle growth. Oxygen debt and lactate production are two things that lead to an increase in growth hormone production and as such they will have a positive effect on both fat loss and muscle growth.

Weekly work-to-restoration ratio

This refers to the frequency of training compared to the restorative measures used. Quite simply, the more (or more often) you train a muscle group without exceeding your recovery capacities, the more muscle you'll gain. This means that you can train a muscle very often (3+ times per week) using a low volume of work, often (2 times per week) using a moderate volume of work, or infrequently (once a week) using a high volume of work. In most cases, the second option (training each muscle group twice a week using a moderate volume) is the best solution. The weekly work-to-restoration ratio is also influenced by your nutritional status: if you are consuming a caloric deficit your body will not recover as fast and as such, you cannot have as many total training sessions during a week. For example if you are consuming a deficit, you might only be able to train 4 times per week while if you are consuming a caloric surplus, you might be able to have 6 weekly workouts. In both cases you can still train each muscle group twice a week but a lower nutritional intake should mean less total weekly workouts. Finally, this weekly ratio can be influenced by your work capacity. If you have a greater tolerance for intense physical work (mesomorphs and meso-endomorphs with an important training experience) you will be able to handle more frequent training sessions or more daily volume than someone with a low work capacity. So as you can see, it's hard to recommend a universal weekly work-to-rest ratio, but as a rule of thumb you should strive to increase the amount of work performed per week as you increase your training experience and thus your work capacity.

Key points

1. Always try to maximize the intraset work-to-rest ratio by avoiding pauses between reps, making sure that you are tensing your muscles maximally during the eccentric portion of the movement, and generating as much force/acceleration as possible on each concentric reps.

2. Try to induce an oxygen debt after each set. The oxygen debt is a good sign that you worked close to your limit and that the set was productive.

3. Shoot for an incomplete recovery between sets. Wait long enough to be able to give a good effort, but not so long that you're breathing normalize.

4. Start by training each muscle group twice a week using a moderate volume. Depending on your nutritional intake and your body type you should split the weekly volume in 4-6 sessions. The fewer calories you consume, the less weekly sessions you should have.

Examples of good weekly training splits

While I would suggest starting by training each muscle group twice a week (and adjust the frequency depending on how your body is reacting) the actual number of training sessions per week will depend on your own capacity to tolerate physical stress, your nutritional intake, and the level of non-training related stress you are under each day. Obviously the less stress you are under, and the better nourished you are, the more weekly training sessions you can have.

Individuals with an ideal recovery situation (low level of stress, consuming a caloric excess, good tolerance for physical work) can train 5 or 6 times per week. For these individuals, any one of these training splits can be used:

Split option 1

Day 1: Quadriceps and Chest
Day 2: Back and Hamstrings
Day 3: Shoulders and Arms
Day 4: Chest and Quadriceps
Day 5: Hamstrings and Back
Day 6: Arms and Shoulders
Day 7: OFF

Split option 2

Day 1: Chest and Back
Day 2: Quadriceps and Hamstrings
Day 3: Shoulders and Arms
Day 4: Back and Chest
Day 5: Hamstrings and Quadriceps
Day 6: Arms and Shoulders
Day 7: OFF

Split option 3

Day 1: Chest, Triceps and Shoulders
Day 2: Quadriceps and Hamstrings
Day 3: Back and Biceps
Day 4: Chest, Triceps and Shoulders
Day 5: Hamstrings and Quadriceps
Day 6: Back and Biceps
Day 7: OFF

Split option 4

Day 1: Chest, Quadriceps and Shoulders
Day 2: Back and Biceps
Day 3: Hamstrings and Triceps
Day 4: OFF
Day 5: Quadriceps, Chest and Triceps
Day 6: Back and Biceps
Day 7: OFF

Individuals with a decent recovery situation (moderate stress levels, sufficient caloric intake, adequate work capacity); this includes the majority of the population, should train 4 times per week. The following splits are adequate for that type of frequency:

Split option 5

Day 1: Quadriceps, Chest and Triceps
Day 2: Hamstrings, Back and Biceps
Day 3: OFF
Day 4: Chest, Quadriceps, Shoulders and Triceps
Day 5: OFF
Day 6: Back, Hamstrings and Biceps
Day 7: OFF

Split option 6

Day 1: Lower Body
Day 2: Upper body
Day 3: OFF
Day 4: Lower body
Day 5: OFF
Day 6: Upper body
Day 7: OFF

Those with a lousy recovery situation (high stress levels, severe caloric deficit, and low work capacity) should train 3 times per week. The following split is adequate for that frequency:

Split option 7

Day 1: Whole body
Day 2: OFF
Day 3: Lower body
Day 4: OFF
Day 5: Upper body
Day 6: OFF
Day 7: OFF

The important thing to remember is that you should strive to hit each muscle group twice per week (some muscle groups receiving a lot of indirect stimulation, like shoulders, can be trained only once a week) and the total number of weekly training sessions will depend on your recovery situation.

PRINCIPLE 9
Select the most effective exercises for each muscle group

Introduction

To stimulate a maximum amount of growth in your muscles you should select the best exercises for each targeted muscle group. While this may seem obvious, there is actually very little information regarding what are the best exercises. And when we finally find such information it's often based on the personal preferences of the author/coach. Just because a supposed training "authority" advocate a certain lift, doesn't automatically make that exercise effective. To make a good exercise selection we must understand what principles govern muscle recruitment; we must also consider the objective of the exercise. When it comes to building muscle mass we have three categories of movements:

1. **Activation exercises**: movements aimed at increasing neural activation, making the nervous system more efficient at recruiting the targeted muscle group. The activation exercise itself won't stimulate a lot (if any) muscle growth, but it will make all the subsequent movements more effective. These movements are basically used to "wake-up" the nervous system. Unstable exercises fall into that category.

2. **Potentiation exercises**: Potentiation means "to make more potent". These exercises are similar in objective to the activation ones in that they increase neural efficiency. However it does so specifically by targeting the fast-twitch fibers (HTMUs) and improving your CNS' capacity to recruit them. Explosive lifts and plyometric drills are the main exercises in that category. Once again, these lifts are not prime muscle-builders (although they are more effective in that regard than activation exercises) but they will increase the efficacy of any subsequent training.

3. **Stimulation exercises**: These are our bread and butter lifts! The movements that will stimulate the most muscle growth. To be effective, a stimulation exercise must revolve around the target muscle's function; it must make biomechanical sense. It should also include a loaded stretch for the targeted muscle group: a stretched muscle during the eccentric phase is an activated muscle during the concentric phase. An exercise in which the targeted muscle is not put under stretch will not stimulate maximum muscle growth.

Exercise selection

In this section I will present the most effective activation, potentiation and stimulation movements for each muscle group. Proper exercise selection is the first step towards building an effective training program. Then the application of the principles already described so far in this book to each of the selected exercises will make sure that you are doing an optimal job at stimulating muscle growth. So without further adieu, here are the top exercises for each muscle group.

Chest activation exercises

As it was noted earlier, when using instability to increase muscle recruitment for the chest muscles, that unstable surface must be under the hands. Making the lower body and core unstable (either by having the feet on a swiss ball, or by sitting on one) while the upper body is stable will not be effective at increasing pectoral recruitment (it will increase the demands on core stability, but this is not what we're after).

Exercise 1. Push up hands on one swiss ball

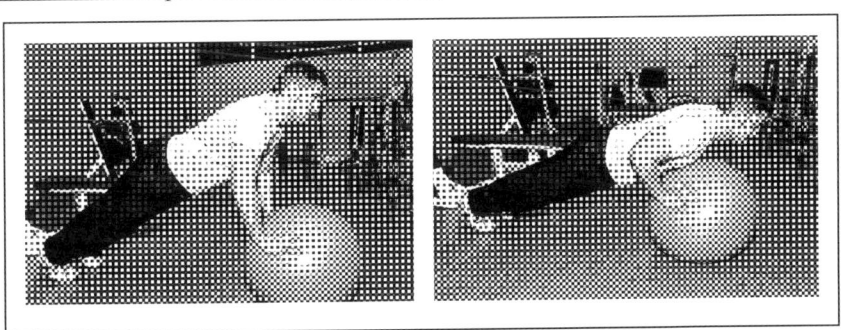

Key point(s): Go down low, but do not touch the ball with your chest, this will remove tension from the pectorals. At the top position, squeeze your pectorals and relax your upper back (to allow for a lateral movement of the scapula).

Exercise 2. Push up hands on two swiss balls

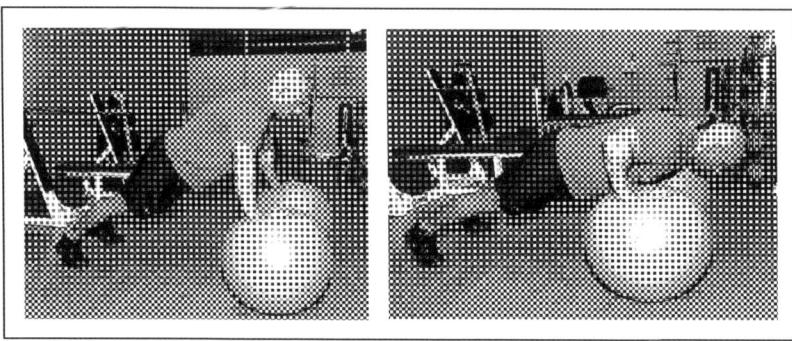

Key point(s): Go down low, but do not touch any of the balls with your chest, this will remove tension from the pectorals. At the top position, squeeze your pectorals and relax your upper back (to allow for a lateral movement of the scapula).

Exercise 3. Push up hands on two wobble boards

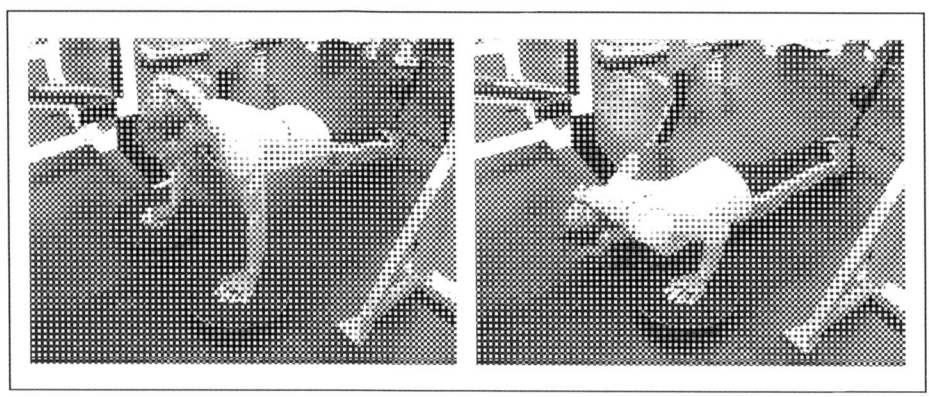

Key point(s): At the top position, squeeze your pectorals and relax your upper back (to allow for a lateral movement of the scapula).

Exercise 4. Push up hands on a swiss ball, single-leg support
Key point(s): Same as with previous movements plus keep hips properly aligned during the whole movement.

Exercise 5. Push up hands on two swiss balls, single-leg support

Key point(s): Same as with previous movements plus keep hips properly aligned during the whole movement.

Exercise 6. Push up hands on two wobble boards, single-leg support

Key point(s): At the top position, squeeze your pectorals and relax your upper back (to allow for a lateral movement of the scapula). Keep hips properly aligned during the whole movement.

Chest potentiation exercises

These exercises include ballistic movements for the chest. We can use medicine balls, barbells or one's bodyweight as a source of resistance and the objective is to project that source of resistance.

Exercise 7. Medicine ball throw from chest

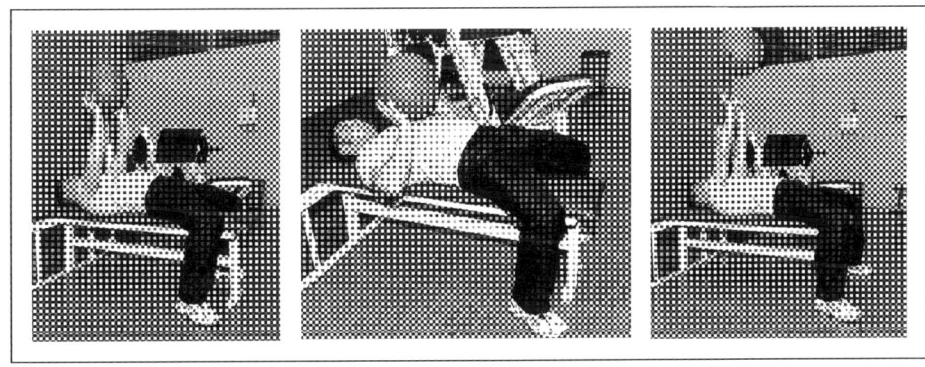

Key point(s): The most important aspect of this exercise is to project the ball with as much power as you can. However even if your primary goal is to throw the ball high, you should still focus on fully contracting the pectorals as you throw the ball in the air.

Exercise 8. Power push up

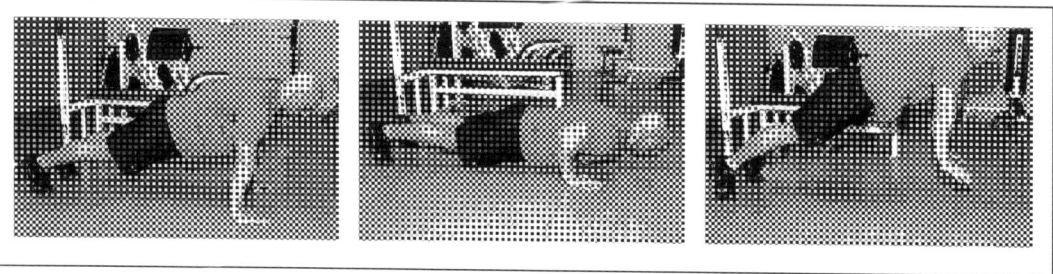

Key point(s): The most important aspect of this exercise is to project your body upwards with as much power as you can. If you have problems executing this movement with enough power and explosion, you should start with the next exercise and get back to this one when your level of strength-speed is high enough.

Exercise 9. Incline power push up

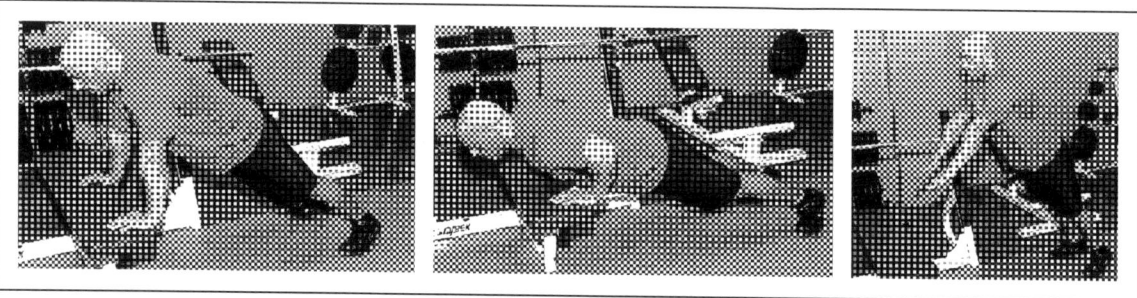

Key point(s): This exercise is the same as the preceding one, but the level of difficulty is lower which will enable less powerful (or heavier) individuals to perform the power push up efficiently.

Exercise 10. Bench throws in Smith machine

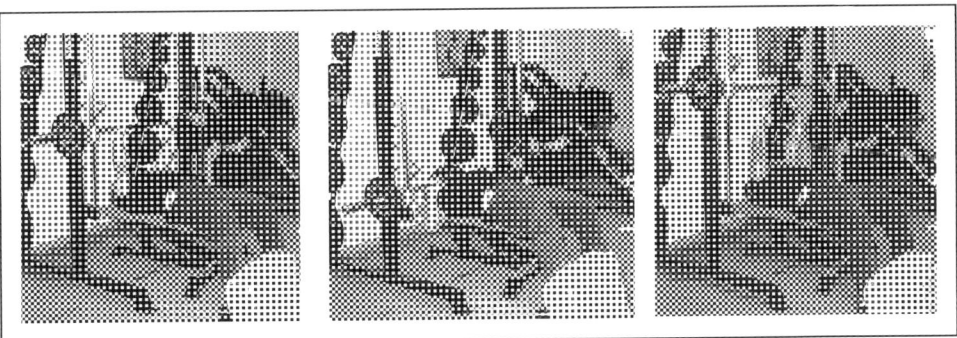

Key point(s): The most important aspect of this exercise is to project the bar with as much power as you can. However even if your primary goal is to throw the bar high, you should still focus on fully contracting the pectorals as you throw the ball in the air. Use around 20-30% of your maximum bench press for this exercise.

Exercise 11. Depth push up

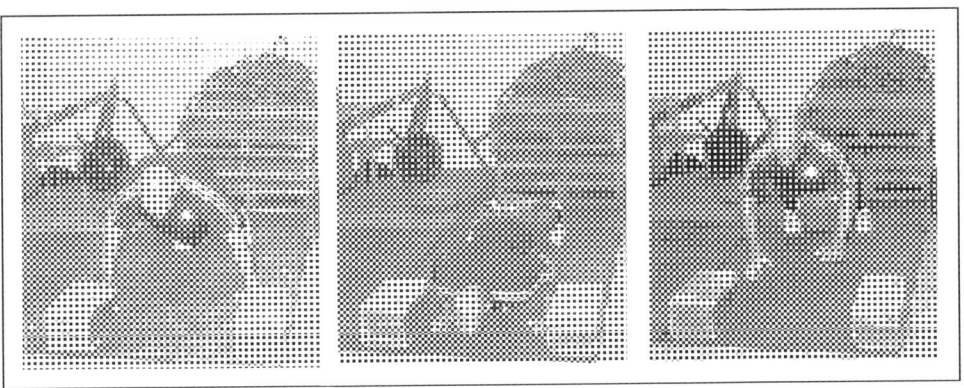

Key point(s): The most important aspect of this exercise is to project your body upwards with as much power as you can. Another important one is to minimize ground contact time; immediately as your hands touch the floor, project yourself upwards. This means leaning with the arms already bent rather than landing with the arms straight then lowering yourself down.

Exercise 12. Whole-body power push up

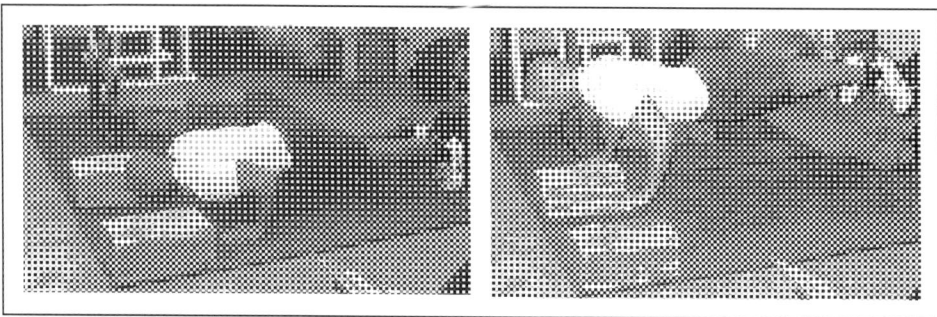

Key point(s): This exercise is very similar to the regular power push up with the difference that you project your whole body in the air. This requires a very good core stability and hip strength.

Exercise 13. Whole-body depth power push up

Key point(s): This exercise is similar to the depth push up with the exception that upon landing on the floor, you project your whole body in the air, not just your torso.

Chest stimulation exercises

To properly stimulate the pectoral muscles and thus making them grow optimally we must select exercises that will allow us to focus on that muscle and to stretch it under load. Remember the third principle we discussed: take advantage of a loaded prestretch of the target muscle. In that regard, a board press (movement used by powerlifters) is fine and well to build bench pressing strength, but it is far from being a good chest exercise.

Exercise 14. Incline dumbbell press

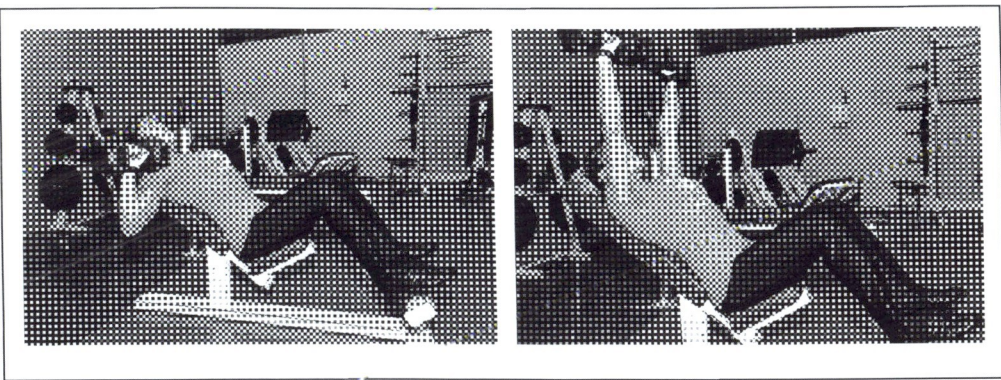

Key point(s): Keep the chest puffed out as much as possible (this will allow you to stretch it more at the bottom position). Lower the dumbbells with the elbows flared out to maximally stretch the pectorals and lift the dumbbells up. Do not turn the dumbbells as you press them, this is both unnecessary and potentially dangerous. Do not bang the dumbbells together, but come as close to touching them as possible.

Exercise 15. Incline hammer dumbbell press

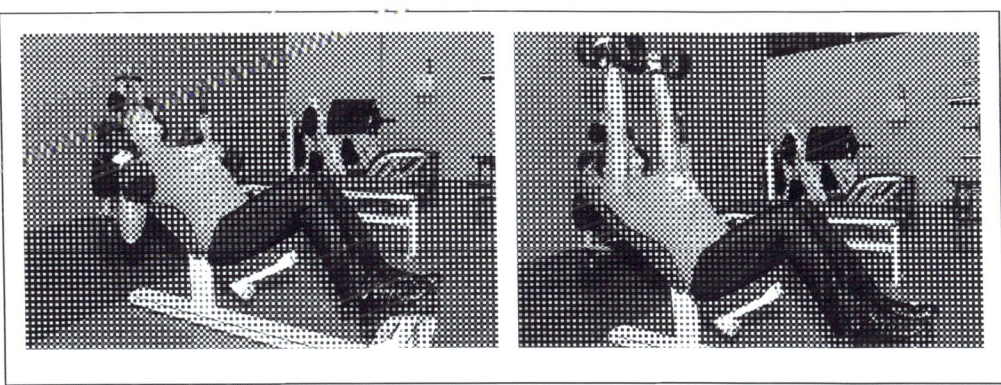

Key point(s): Even though you are using a hammer/neutral grip, still flare your elbows out somewhat, do not keep them close to your body as this will lead to more triceps but less pectoral activation. Do not turn the dumbbells as you press them, this is both unnecessary and potentially dangerous. Do not bang the dumbbells together, but come as close to touching them as possible.

Exercise 16. Dumbbell bench press

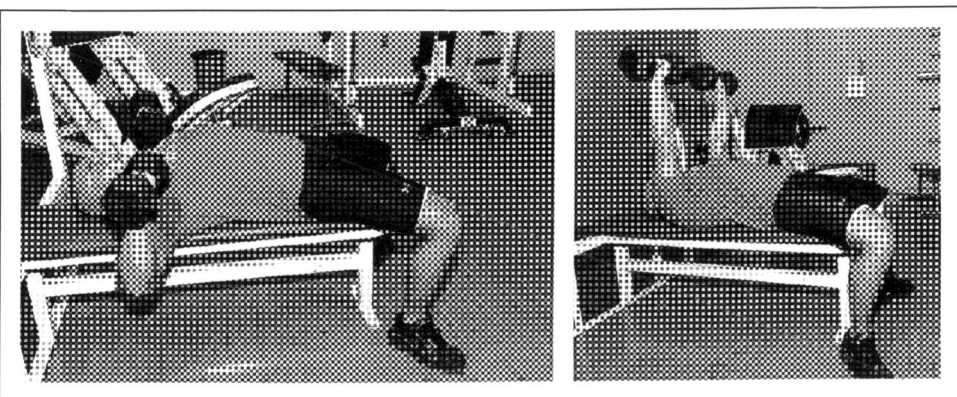

Key point(s): Keep the chest puffed out as much as possible (this will allow you to stretch it more at the bottom position). Lower the dumbbells with the elbows flared out to maximally stretch the pectorals and lift the dumbbells up. Do not turn the dumbbells as you press them, this is both unnecessary and potentially dangerous. Do not bang the dumbbells together, but come as close to touching them as possible.

Exercise 17. Decline dumbbell press

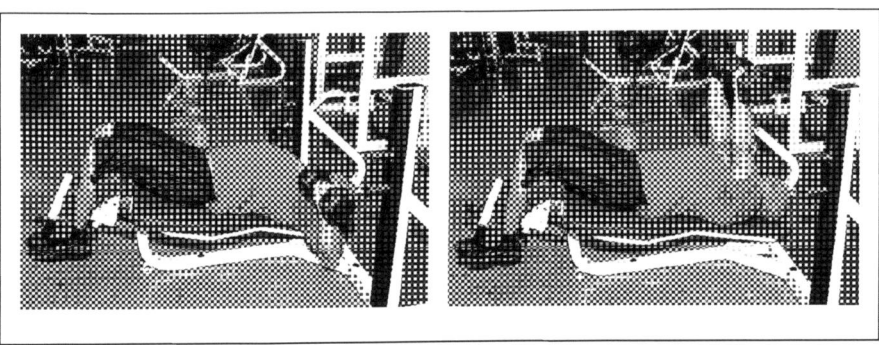

Key point(s): Keep the chest puffed out as much as possible (this will allow you to stretch it more at the bottom position). Lower the dumbbells with the elbows flared out to maximally stretch the pectorals and lift the dumbbells up. Do not turn the dumbbells as you press them, this is both unnecessary and potentially dangerous. Do not bang the dumbbells together, but come as close to touching them as possible. The more dominant your shoulders are, the greater should the incline be.

Exercise 18. Alternate DB bench press from high position

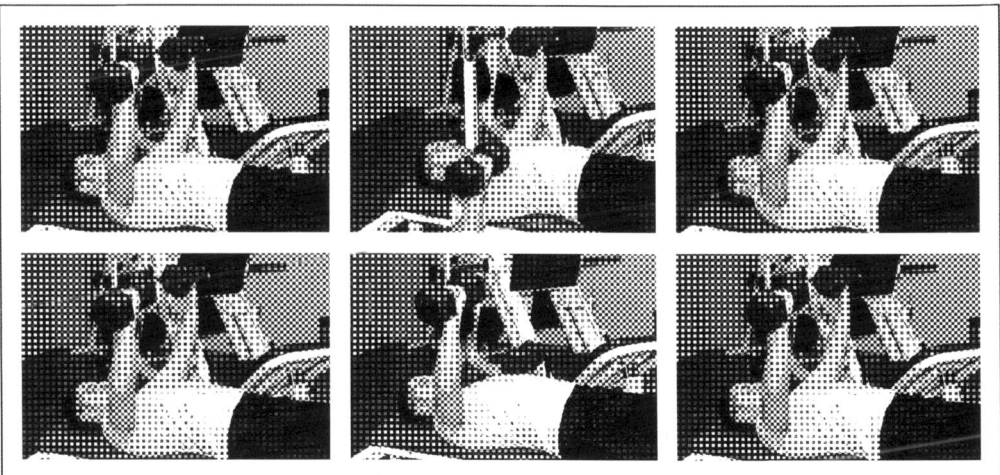

Key point(s): You exercise one limb at a time. As your perform the movement with your right limb, the left arm stays extended (but not locked). Change arms on every repetition. This exercise can either be done as a stimulation exercise or as a potentiation exercise if a light weight is used and as many speed reps are performed for a prescribed time.

Exercise 19. Decline flies

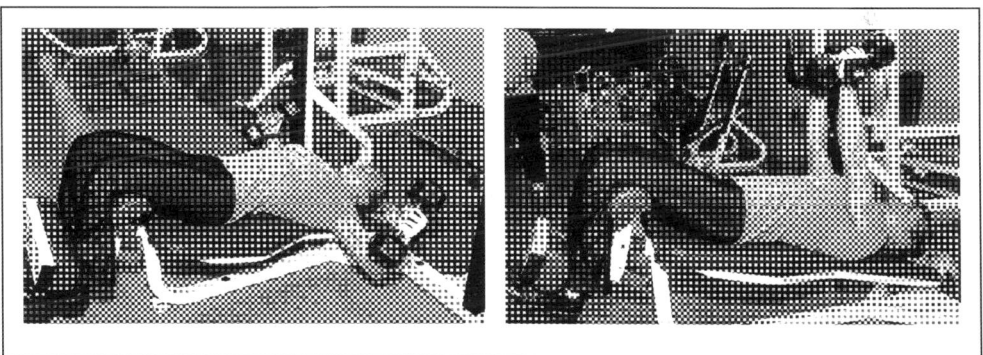

Key point(s): As with all the chest exercises it is important to keep the chest puffed out and the flare the elbows out to stretch the pectoral muscles. In the low position bent the arms at a 90 degrees angle to maximally stretch the chest while keeping stress off of the elbow joint. Note: can also be performed with two low pulleys.

Exercise 20. Flat flies

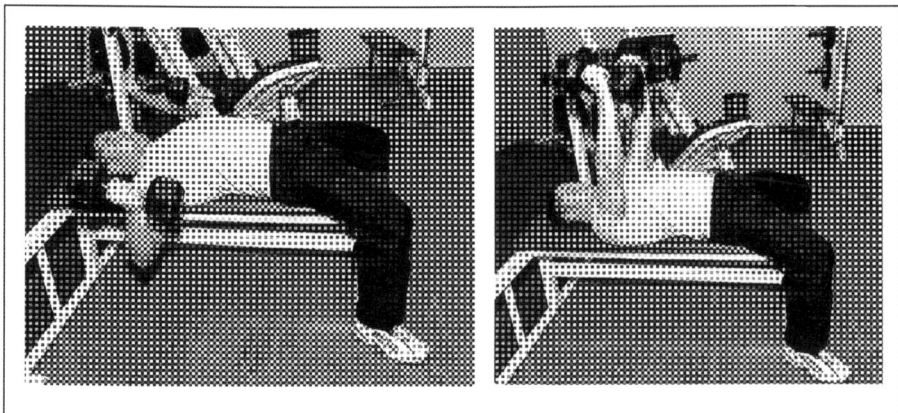

Key point(s): As with all the chest exercises it is important to keep the chest puffed out and the flare the elbows out to stretch the pectoral muscles. In the low position bent the arms at a 90 degrees angle to maximally stretch the chest while keeping stress off of the elbow joint. Note: can also be performed with two low pulleys.

Exercise 21. Unilateral cable cross-over

Key point(s): I like this variation of the cross-over because it has a stronger postural component to it. You really have to work the glutes and obliques hard to keep a stable position. Always aim for the most important stretch possible at the top position. At the top, bend the elbows somewhat to reduce elbow stress.

Exercise 22. High-to-low cable cross-over

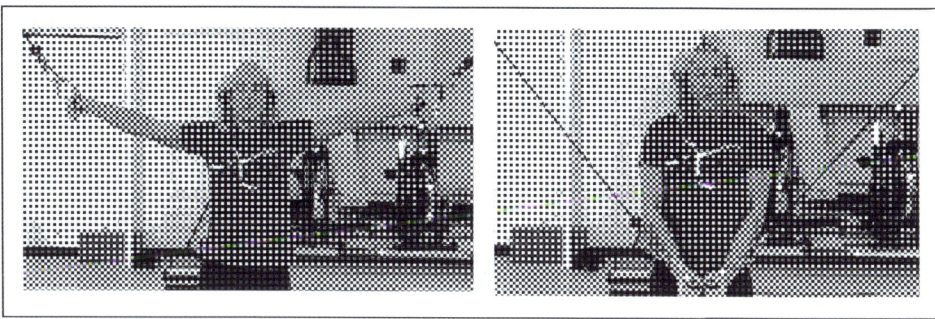

Key point(s): Keep the torso straight during the movement (do not bend forward). Get a maximum stretch at the top and bring the arms down toward your hips.

Exercise 23. High-to-high cable cross-over

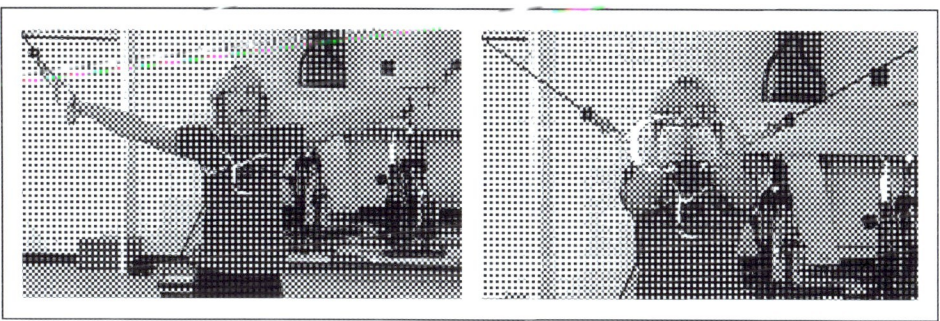

Key point(s): Keep the torso straight during the movement (do not bend forward). Get a maximum stretch at the top and bring the arms in front of your face. At the finish position, push forward to get a maximum pectoral contraction.

Exercise 24. Decline bench press

Key point(s): Like with the dumbbell variation of this exercise, keep the chest puffed out and flare the elbows as you lower the bar. It's important to bring the bar toward the middle of your chest (of ever to the upper portion) to get a maximal stretch. Most peoples want to use too much weight on this exercise and lower the bar down to the lower portion of their chest so that they can lift more weight. But this doesn't optimally stimulate the pectorals.

What ... no bench press?!
As you probably noticed, I didn't include the regular bench press in my "best exercises" list. The reason is quite simple actually: the regular bench press is a lousy pectoral exercise for most individuals. I have rarely seen someone who focuses only on the bench press have good pectoral development. Most of the time, these individuals will have big triceps and/or deltoids, but a very incomplete chest development. The strongest bench pressers normally have underdeveloped pectorals (compared to their other pressing muscles) unless they also perform better chest exercises in their program.

The powerlifting bench press is first and foremost a triceps exercise. To make the bench press and effective pectoral movement we must use a wide grip, flare the elbows out and bring the bar down to the collar-bone (known as a neck press). However this way you cannot use as much weight as with a regular bench press and ego is quick to jump in and you revert back to a less effective variation of the bench press. This is why I didn't include it in my list. But if you are able to leave your ego at the door and perform a proper neck press, then it can be a useful addition to a good pectoral program.

Back activation exercises

There are not many activation exercises for the back, at least not as much as for the chest for example. The inverted row variations performed with the feet on a swiss ball are very good for that purpose, and contrary to most activation exercises they are actually quite effective as growth stimulation exercise too.

Exercise 25. Inverted row with a pronation grip

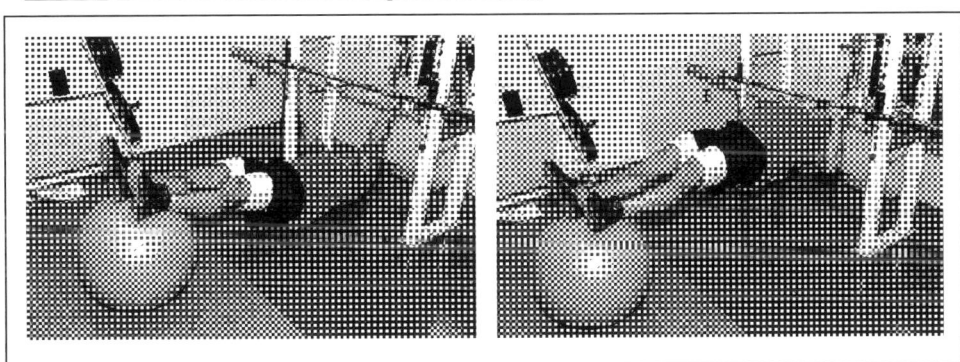

Key point(s): Get a full back stretch in the low position. Really focus on stretching the back, not the arms. Keep the hips, feet and shoulders aligned during the whole movement.

Exercise 26. Inverted row with a suppination grip

Key point(s): Get a full back stretch in the low position. Really focus on stretching the back, not the arms. Keep the hips, feet and shoulders aligned during the whole movement.

Back potentiation exercises

Just like with the previous two activation exercises, the back potentiation drills can stimulate a lot of muscle growth by themselves. They rely either on explosive movements or complex back drills where stability is important.

Exercise 27. Alternate floor Hex DB row

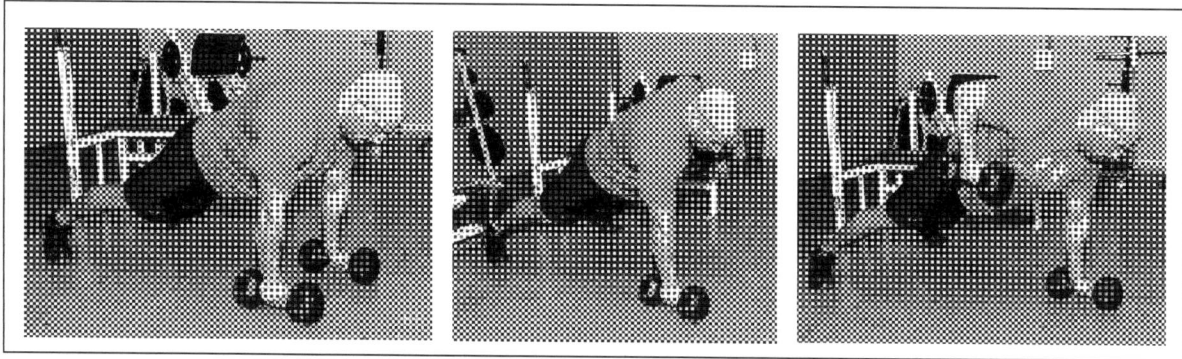

Key point(s): Keep the torso solid by keeping the obliques and glutes tight, do not let the hips drop down towards the floor and do not keep them high-up either. Avoid twisting & turning of the trunk and hips during the set. Use light weights for speed reps as a potentiating exercise and heavier weights for growth stimulation.

Exercise 28. Alternate floor kettlebell row

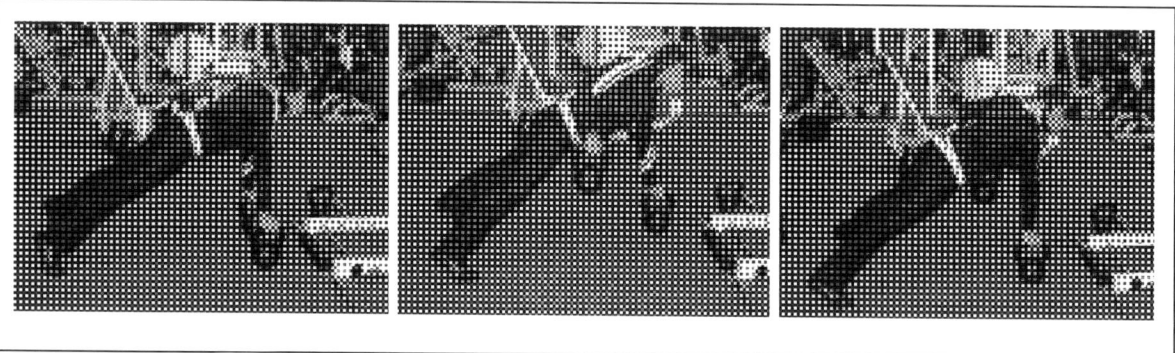

Key point(s): Keep the torso solid by keeping the obliques and glutes tight, do not let the hips drop down towards the floor and do not keep them high-up either. Avoid twisting &

turning of the trunk and hips during the set. Use light weights for speed reps as a potentiating exercise and heavier weights for growth stimulation.

Exercise 29. Alternate standing DB row

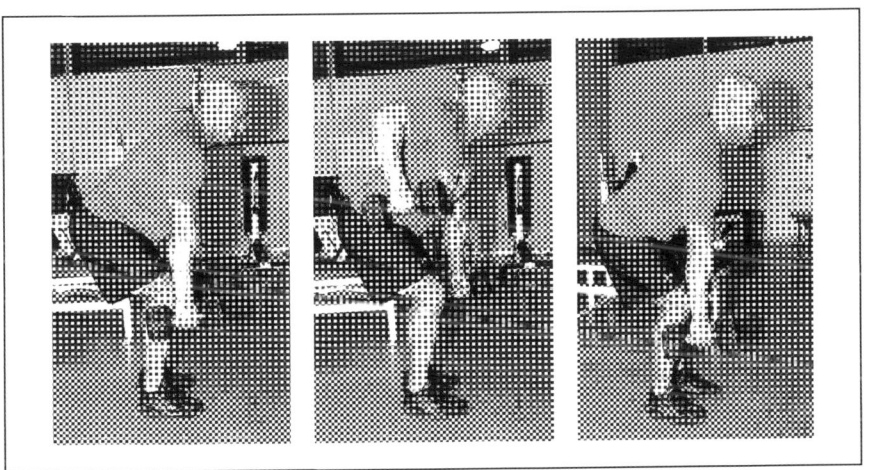

Key point(s): Keep the lower back arched and the abdominals tight. Avoid twisting & turning of the trunk and hips during the set. Use light weights for speed reps as a potentiating exercise and heavier weights for growth stimulation.

Exercise 30a. and 30b. Power clean from blocks or from hang

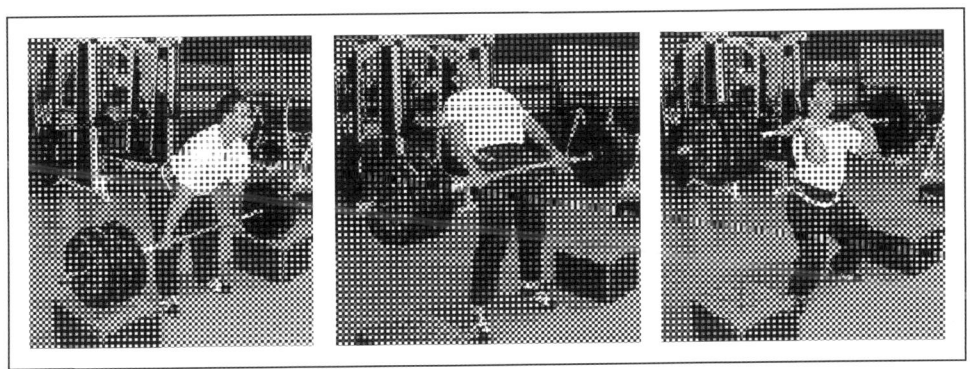

Key point(s): Keep a beach position (chest out) during the whole set. Keep the bar close to the body. Explode upwards using the back, traps and legs. If you don't have access to a coach and are not knowledgeable about the Olympic lifts, I suggest using other potentiating movements.

Exercise 31a. and 31b. Power snatch from blocks or from hang

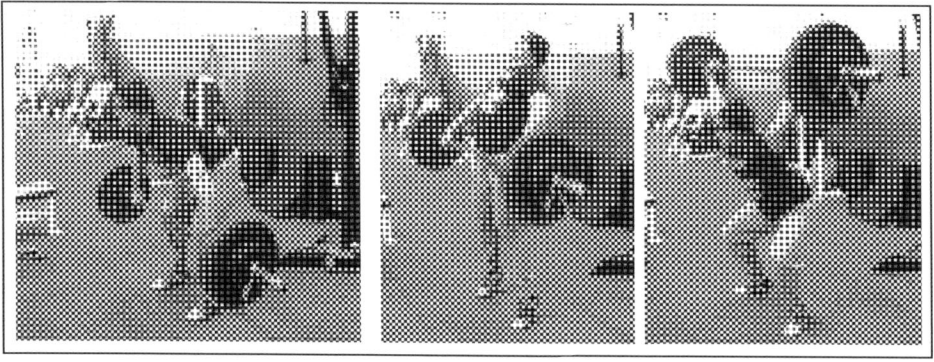

Key point(s): Keep a beach position (chest out) during the whole set. Keep the bar close to the body. Explode upwards using the back, traps and legs. If you don't have access to a coach and are not knowledgeable about the Olympic lifts, I suggest using other potentiating movements.

Back stimulation exercises

As I already explained, the potentiation and activation exercises for the back can also be used as stimulation exercises if the load is adjusted accordingly. However there are several other great back exercises out there. Specifically there are three types of back movements: vertical pulling, horizontal pulling and "pullover" movements. All three share one common denominator: to be maximally effective, the back muscles must be fully stretched before starting the concentric portion of the movement. You must stretch/open up the back, not stretch the biceps or shoulders. Remember that the muscle that is stretched the most is the one that will be recruited to the greatest extent.

Exercise 32 1-arm dumbbell rowing

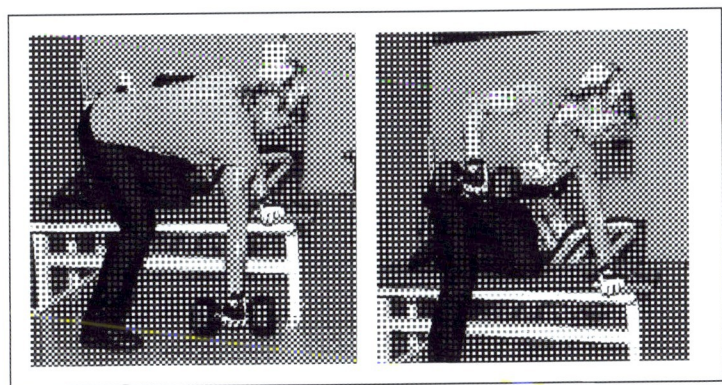

Key point(s): Really stretch/open up the back at the bottom position. The dumbbell should be in line with the shoulders. Then you pull it toward your hip, focusing on the back muscles. You will notice how the elbow is lifted high but the arm is not bent more than 90 degrees. If the arm is bent more than that, the arm flexors will receive the most stimulation, not the back.

Exercise 33. Chest-supported DB rowing

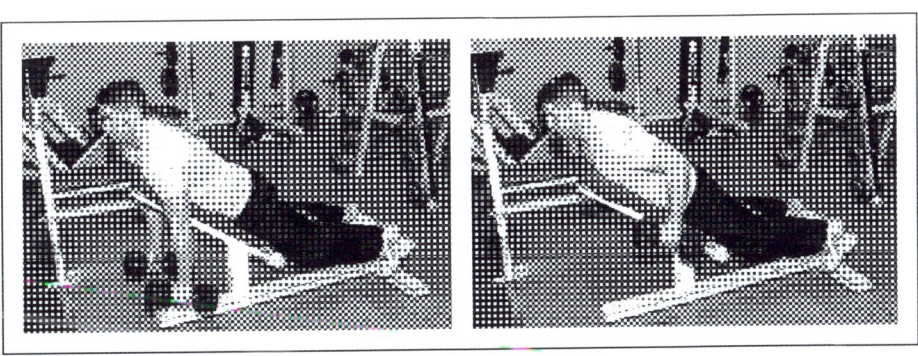

Key point(s): The same coaching points as with exercise 32 applies for this one: stretch the back, pull toward the hips, and do not bend elbows more than 90 degrees.

Exercise 34. Corner rowing

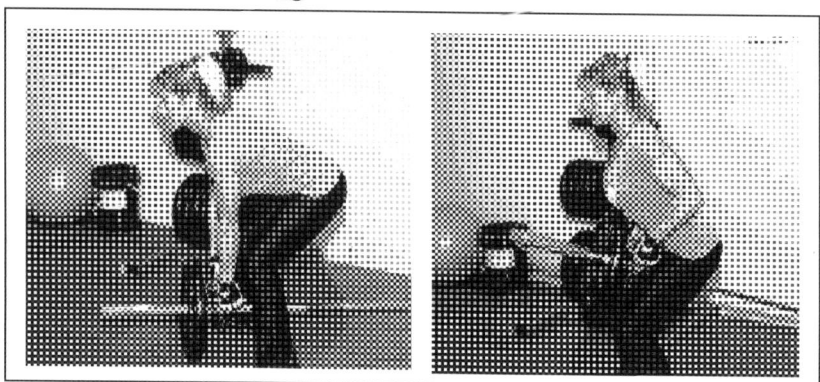

Key point(s): I like this exercise because it's next to impossible to "*overpull*" with the arms because of the restricted range of motion and pulling angle. If you really focus on opening up the back in the low position and bringing your shoulders back at the top you will get a tremendous overall back development from this exercise.

Exercise 35. Rope lat pulldown

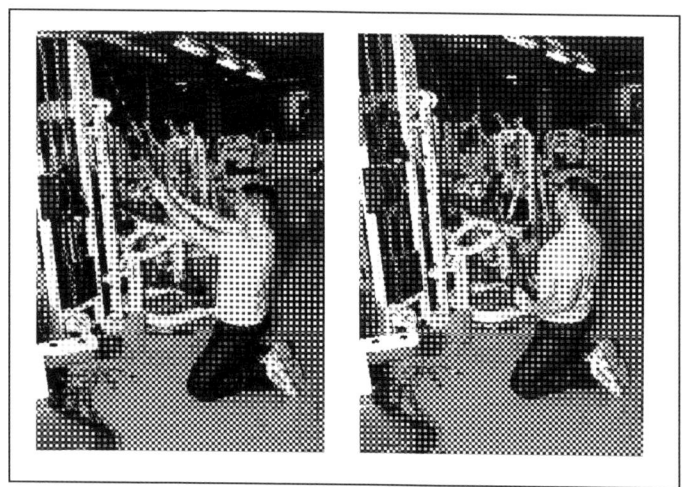

Key point(s): This is the movement that more closely duplicate the complete function of the Latissimus dorsi. Open up the back at the start and pull the rope toward your hips, again avoid bending the elbows more than 90 degrees. At the bottom position really emphasize bringing the shoulders down and back.

Exercise 36. Straight-arms pulldown pronation grip

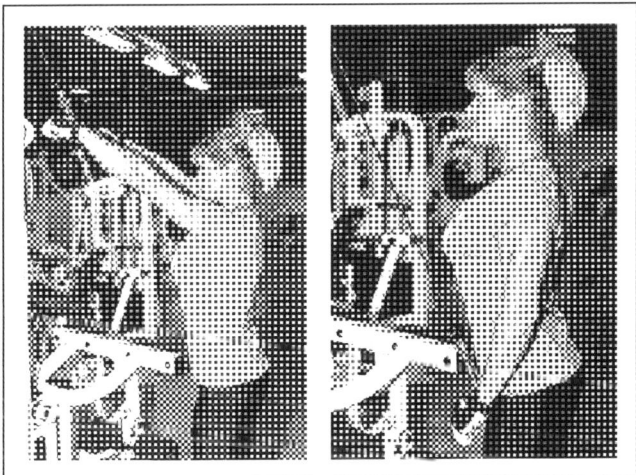

Key point(s): Keep the torso in a proper anatomical position (do not bend forward). Stretch the lats at the top of the movement and bring the handle down low, toward your pelvis. At the bottom position try to bring the shoulders down and back as much as possible.

Exercise 37. Straight-arms pulldown neutral grip

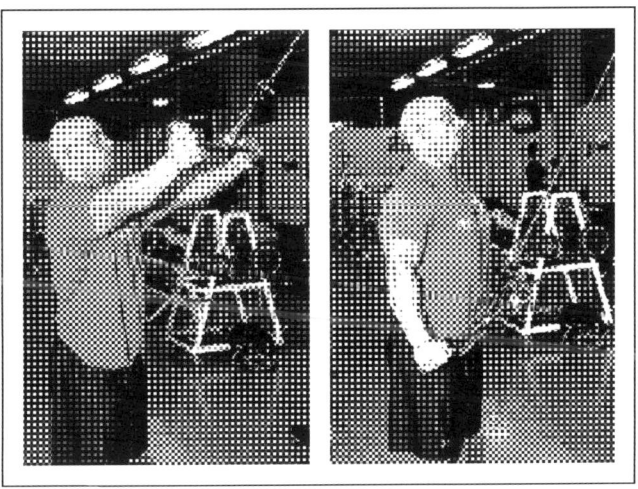

Key point(s): The comments given for exercise 36 applies to this one too.

Exercise 38. 1-arm pulldown

Key point(s): No in the picture Carl isn't doing the movement wrong; at the top position we want to fully stretch the lats but not the biceps. The elbow bent is done on purpose to deemphasize the biceps. This is especially important in this exercise because the arm flexors will tend to dominate this movement more so than many other back exercises. So the key is to stretch the lats as much as possible and bring the elbow down and back as you pull.

Exercise 39. Low-pulley cross rowing

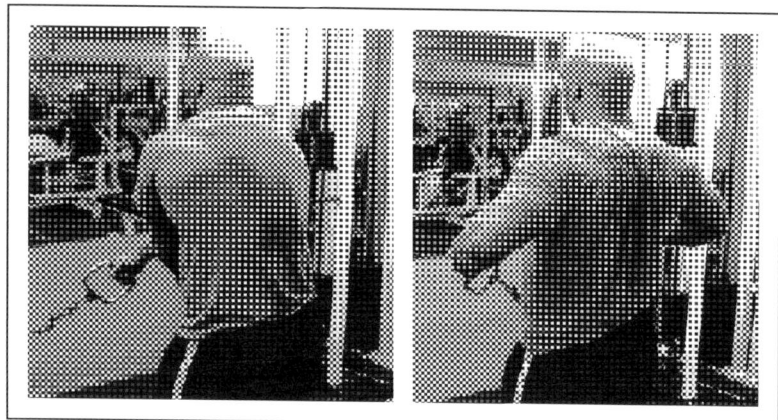

Key point(s): The first key point is the "open up" (stretch) your back in the starting position and to squeeze your shoulder blades together at the fully contracted position. The second one is to keep the elbows bend to a minimum during the pull (to minimize biceps involvement).

Exercise 40. High-pulley cross rowing

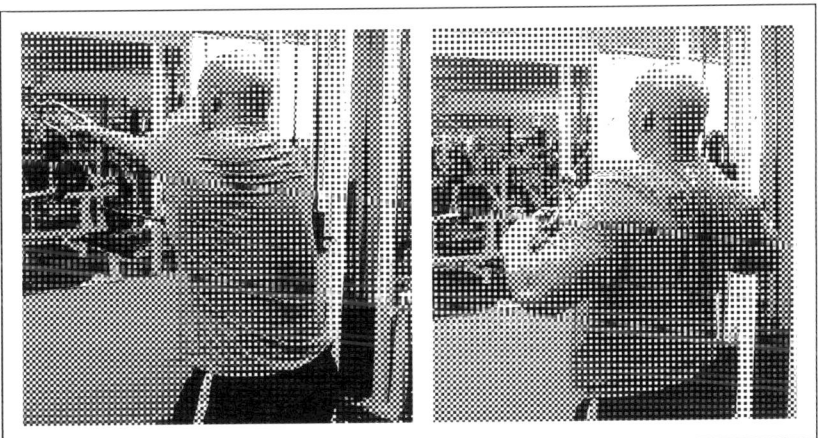

Key point(s): Same as for exercise 39.

Exercise 41. Chin-up

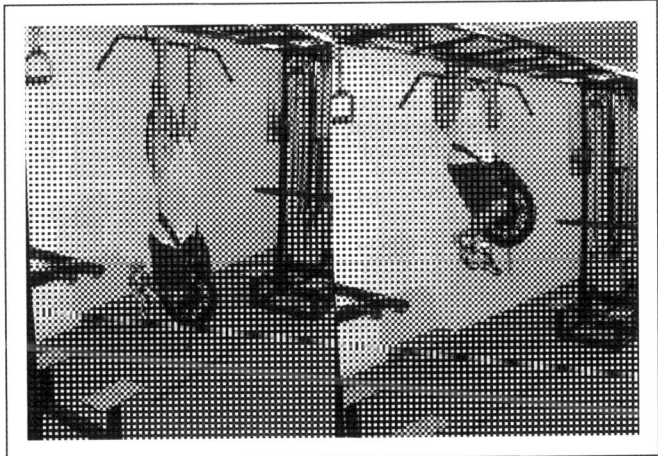

Key point(s): A lot of peoples see the chin-up as the ultimate back exercise, and when it's properly performed it is indeed a very effective exercise. However very few peoples actually perform it correctly; a lot of peoples under stimulate their back and rely and too much arm pull. Some also use bad form and momentum. If you are able to perform this movement properly, focusing most of the stress on your back, then by all means include it in your programs. If not, you are better off with another exercise.

Exercise 42. Lat pulldown torso straight

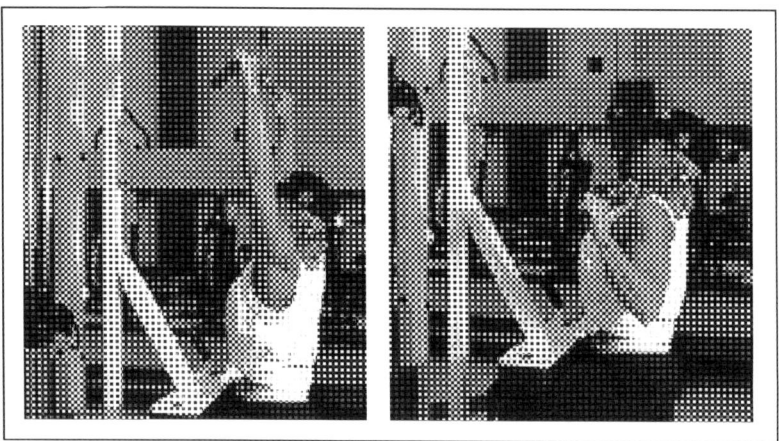

Key point(s): You should try to bring your elbows to your ribs. Unless you are really flexible or have very long limbs, you won't be able to reach your ribs. But it is a good technical cue to shirt the stress to the lats instead of the rhomboids, rear delts and arms. The torso should remain perfectly straight during the whole movement.

Exercise 43. Lat pulldown leaning back

Key point(s): This variation puts a bit more stress on the rhomboids. The key points should be the same as with the preceding exercise.

Exercise 44. Seated row to mid pec line

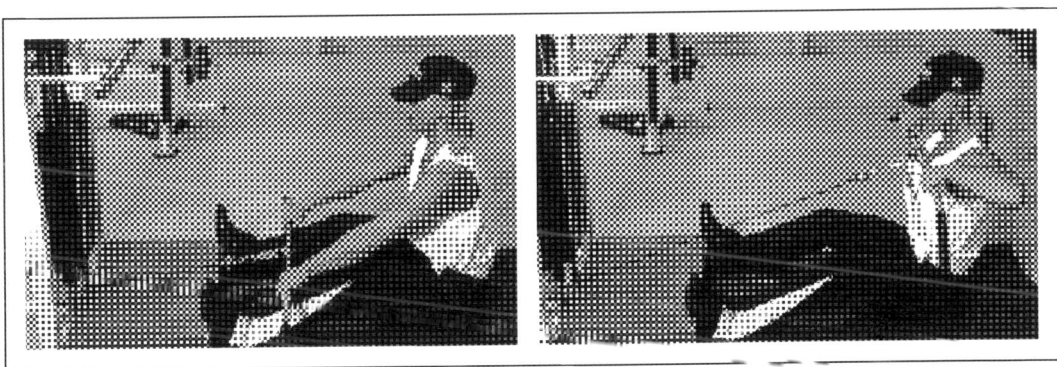

Key point(s): Focus on stretching/opening up the back at the beginning of the movement and pull it toward the middle of your chest. Emphasise bringing the shoulders far back to squeeze the mid portion of the upper back.

Exercise 45. Bent over barbell rowing

Key point(s): Some peoples don't like this exercise because either a) it's not performed correctly (swinging and momentum, arm pull, etc.) or b) involves the lower back too much. While both of these are good point, if form is correct and the lower back is healthy this exercise will be very effective to build upper back size. It allows for a full stretch of the upper back at the beginning of the movement, which as you know is very important. You should pull the bar towards your navel, squeezing the elbows in and bringing your shoulder blades together. While you need to try to accelerate the load during the concentric portion of the movement, do not use momentum created by the legs or lower back.

Exercise 46. 1-arm low-pulley rowing

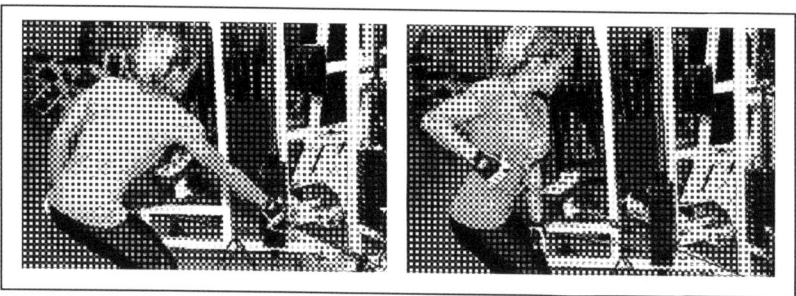

Key point(s): Really stretch the whole upper back in the starting position.

Biceps activation exercises

When it comes to improving biceps activation by the nervous system we can either use a unstable surface or an exercise where the biceps must both act as a stabilizer and a prime mover. To make an unstable exercise effective as increasing biceps activation the source of instability should be directly under the arm; sitting on a swiss ball and doing curls is not a biceps activation exercise (it's a core/abdominal activation exercise). Like with the back, the activation exercises are also decent stimulation ones.

Exercise 47. 1-arm barbell preacher curl

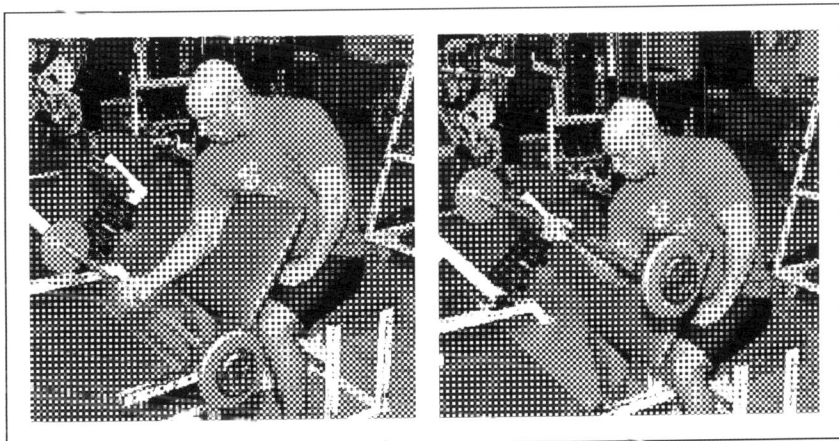

Key point(s): Keep the bar perfectly parallel to the floor at all times. The wrist should be cocked back (extended) or neutral to maximise the stabilizing role of the biceps.

Exercise 48. 1-arm barbell standing curl

Key point(s): Keep the bar perfectly parallel to the floor at all times. The wrist should be cocked back (extended) or neutral to maximise the stabilizing role of the biceps. Maintain a properly aligned posture at all time; do not shift your weight to one side or bend laterally.

Exercise 49. 1-arm swiss ball preacher curl

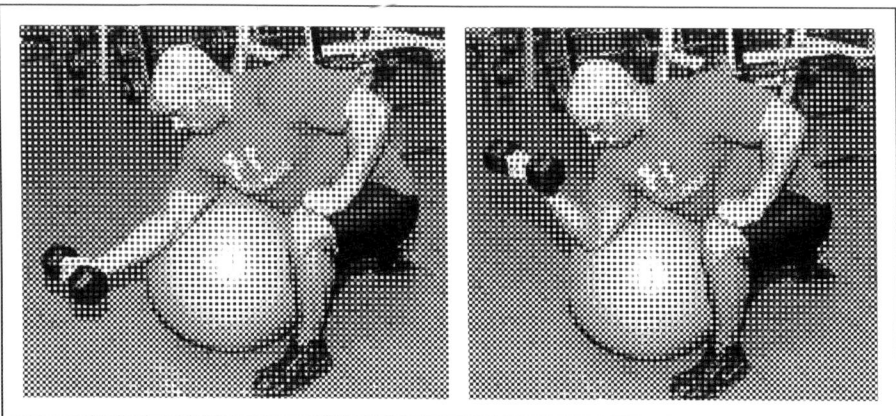

Key point(s): The farther forward and down you put your elbow; the harder this exercise gets.

Biceps stimulation exercises

We don't really have any potentiation exercises specifically for the biceps. On could always perform explosive curls or drop & catch curls, but it is rarely necessary to potentiate the action of the biceps.

The best stimulation exercises for the biceps are a rather limited group; as I already mentioned to be maximally effective an exercise should allow you to stretch the muscle prior to the concentric action. It is impossible to stretch the biceps if you are performing curls at a fixed position because the biceps stretch is limited by the elbow's range of motion. To maximally stretch the biceps you must bring the shoulder back under load (the biceps is also a shoulder flexor). So our selection is pretty small. However to the list of optimal exercises we can also add some more which, although not quite as effective, can have their place in a program.

Exercise 50. Incline dumbbell curl

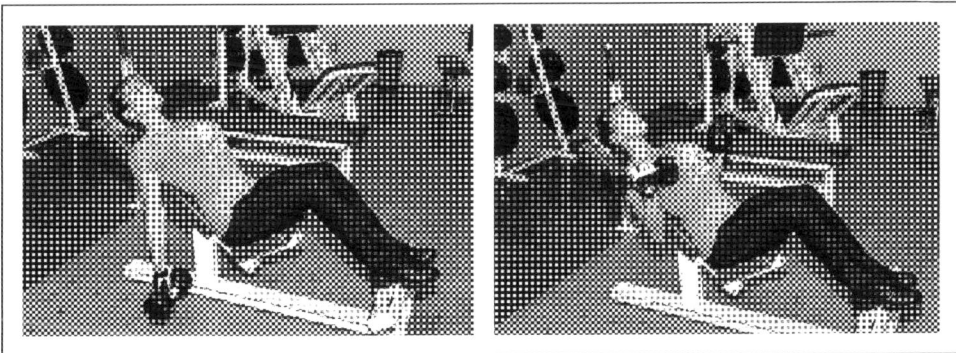

Key point(s): Get a maximum biceps stretch by bringing the arm back at the starting position. As you curl up, simultaneously bring the elbows forward a bit. Do not supinate the weight as you curl it: start with the palms up, end with the palms up. Starting the movement with a hammer grip will stretch a different portion of the biceps (outer portion) than the one targeted by the rest of the exercise (inner portion).

Exercise 51. Incline hammer curl

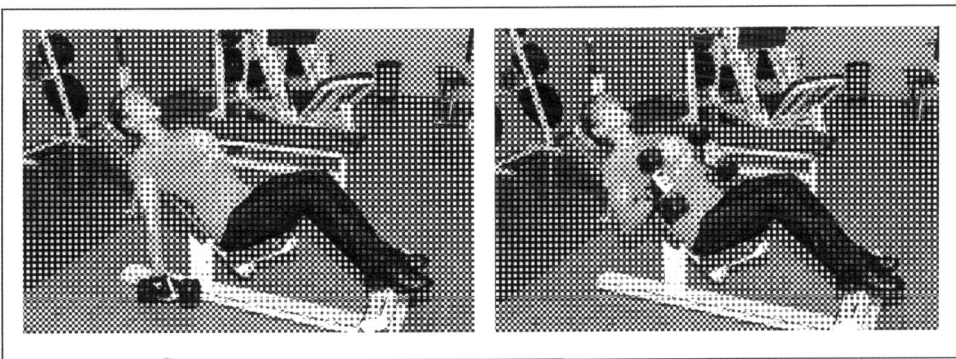

Key point(s): Get a maximum biceps stretch by bringing the arm back at the starting position. As you curl up, simultaneously bring the elbows forward a bit.

Exercise 52. Low pulley stretched curl

Key point(s): Get a maximum biceps stretch by bringing the arm back at the starting position. As you curl up, simultaneously bring the elbows forward a bit. Do not supinate the weight as you curl it: start with the palms up, end with the palms up.

Exercise 53. Low pulley stretched hammer curl

Key point(s): Get a maximum biceps stretch by bringing the arm back at the starting position. As you curl up, simultaneously bring the elbows forward a bit.

Other good biceps stimulation exercises

Exercise 54. Preacher curl

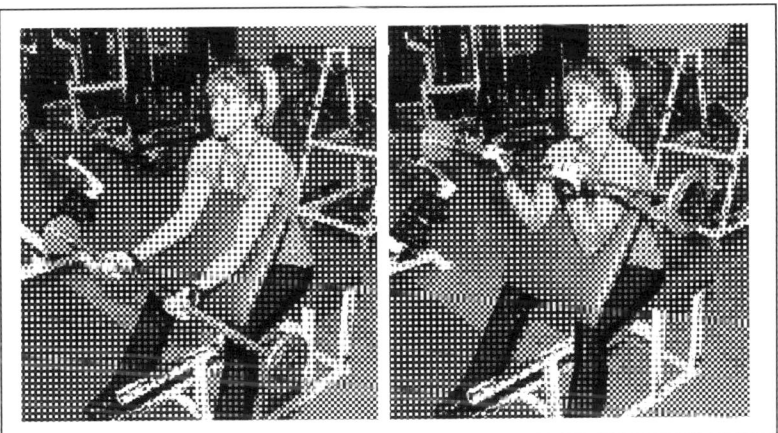

Key point(s): Keep the wrist neutral to focus more of the stress on the biceps. Do not allow the biceps to relax at any time during the movement (flex hard at all time) to compensate for the lack of stretch.

Exercise 55. Barbell curl

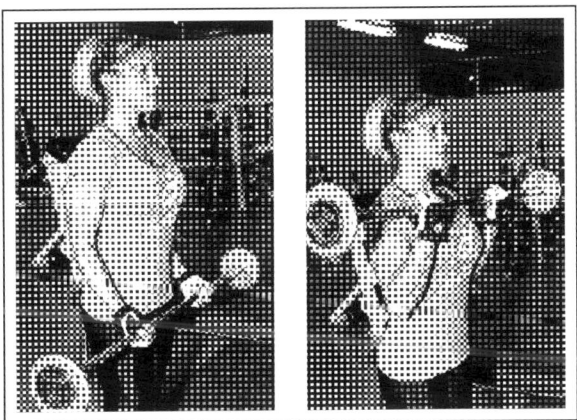

Key point(s): Keep the wrist neutral to focus more of the stress on the biceps. Do not allow the biceps to relax at any time during the movement (flex hard at all time) to compensate for the lack of stretch.

Exercise 56. 1-arm machine preacher curl

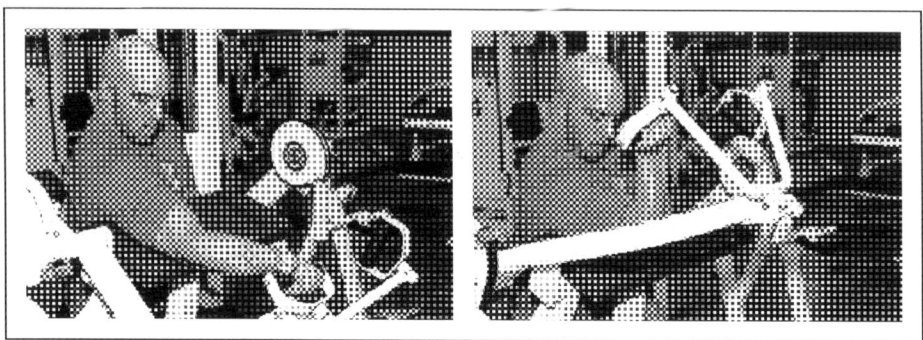

Key point(s): In most cases I'm not a machine nut. But for a small muscle group like the biceps, this machine works very well. I prefer the unilateral version (1-arm); since the machine isn't as efficient as free-weights, the unilateral portion can compensate by increasing muscular activation.

Exercise 57. Machine preacher curl

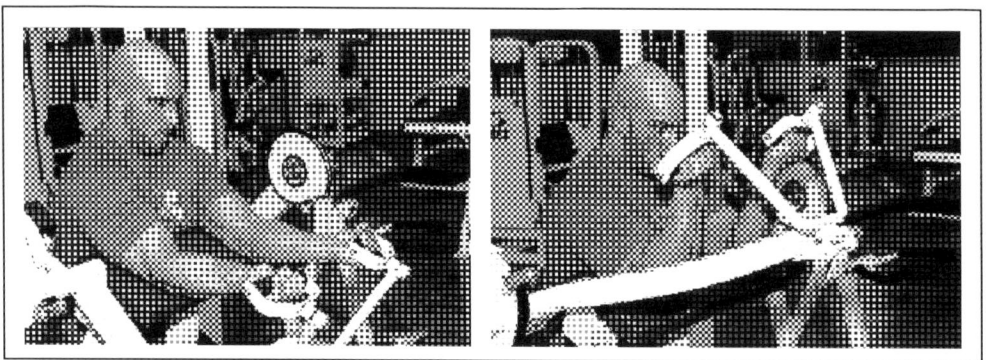

Key point(s): While I prefer the unilateral variation of this exercise; the bilateral one still has its place in a training plan. Really focus on flexing the biceps as hard as you can during the whole movement and on keeping the wrist cocked back or neutral.

Triceps activation and potentiation exercises

The triceps activation and potentiation exercises are essentially the same as those for the chest, but on the triceps variations you keep the elbows closer to the body.

Triceps stimulation exercises

Just like with the biceps, there aren't many optimal triceps exercises. The capacity to stretch that muscle is limited by the mobility of the elbow joint. However since the triceps is also a shoulder flexor, it can be stretched by bringing the upper arm up at the starting position of a triceps movement.

Exercise 58. Overhead barbell triceps extension

Key point(s): Bring the elbows back as far as possible at the starting position. Lack of shoulder mobility might be a problem to some so if you find that this is a problem, you should definitely work on improving the mobility around that joint.

Exercise 59. Overhead dumbbell triceps extension

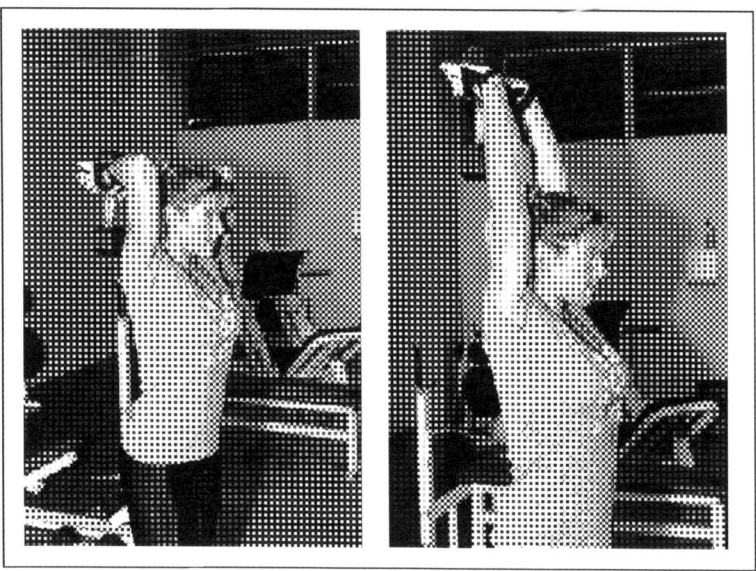

Key point(s): Bring the elbows back as far as possible at the starting position. Lack of shoulder mobility might be a problem to some so if you find that this is a problem, you should definitely work on improving the mobility around that joint.

Exercise 60. 1-arm overhead dumbbell triceps extension

Key point(s): Pretty much everything that applied for the last two exercises are true here too.

Exercise 61. Overhead low-pulley triceps extension

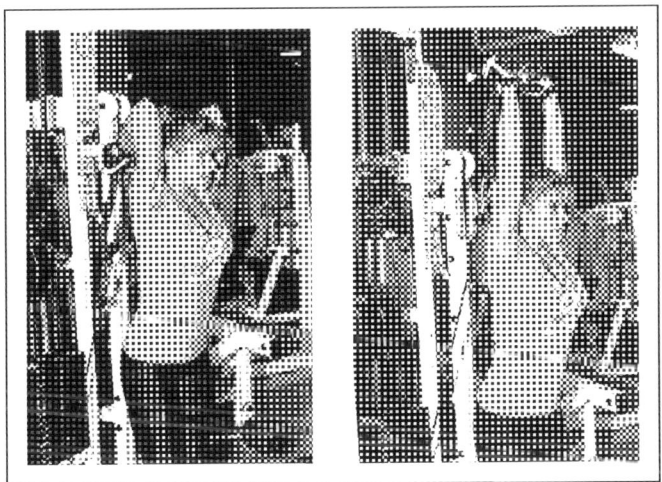

Key point(s): Pretty much everything that applied for the last three exercises are true here too.

Exercise 62. Decline barbell triceps extension

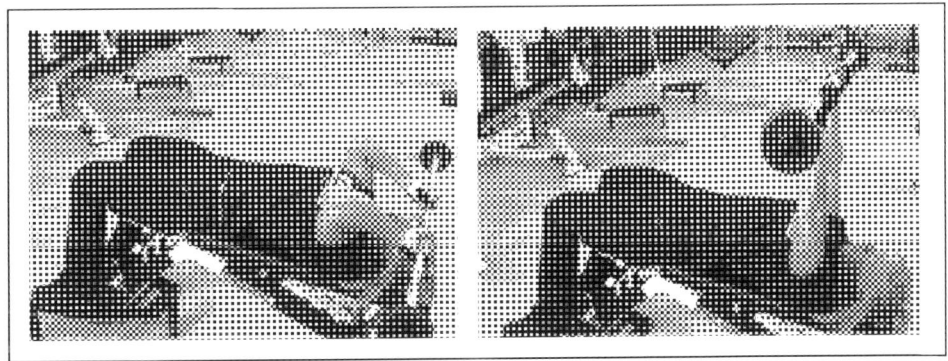

Key point(s): I like decline more so than flat extension work because the angle allows you to get a better loaded stretch of the triceps.

Exercise 63. Decline dumbbell triceps extension

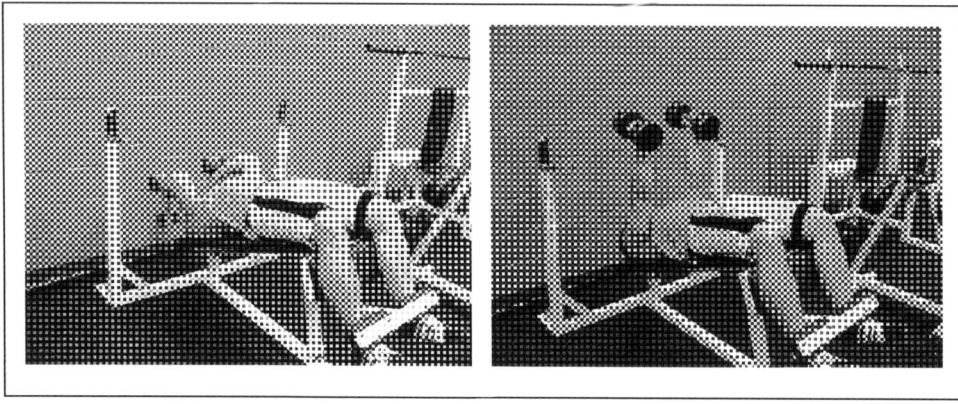

Key point(s): Focus on getting good triceps stretch by bringing the arms back a bit on the way down.

Exercise 64. Close-grip bench press

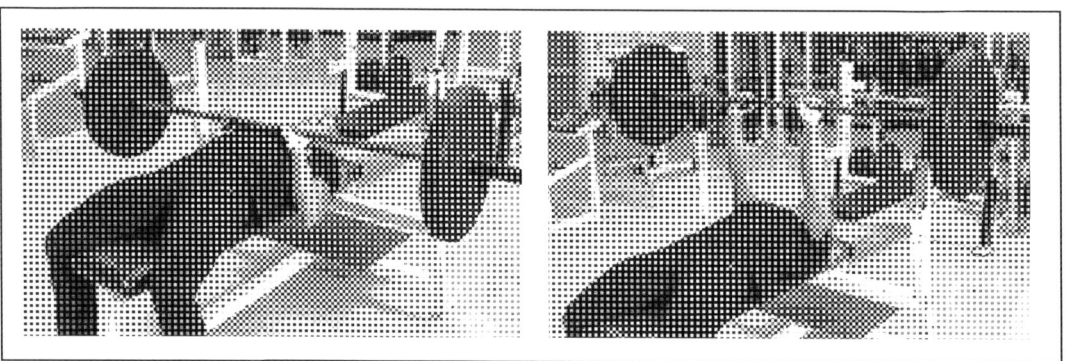

Key point(s): Use a grip that is just inside shoulder width. Keep the elbows close to the body as you lower, and lift the bar.

Other good triceps stimulation exercises

These are not as good as the preceding exercises because the stretch component is less present. However they still represent very effective exercise and can be added to a good program.

Exercise 65. Flat barbell triceps extension

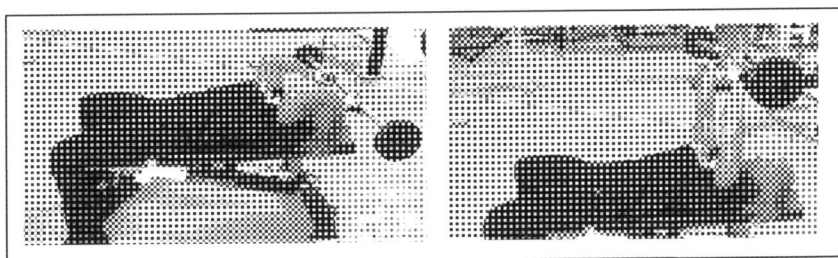

Key point(s): Keep the elbows tucked in and pointing towards the ceiling in the low position.

Exercise 66. Flat dumbbell triceps extension

Key point(s): Keep the elbows tucked in and pointing towards the ceiling in the low position.

Exercise 67. High pulley overhead triceps extension

Key point(s): Keep the elbows tucked in and pointing forward in the starting position.

Exercise 68. High pulley triceps extension

Key point(s): Keep the torso upright (do not bend forward). The elbows should be close to the body during the eccentric portion of the movement and you should try to "split the ropes" at the bottom position.

Exercise 69. 1-arm cross-body triceps extension

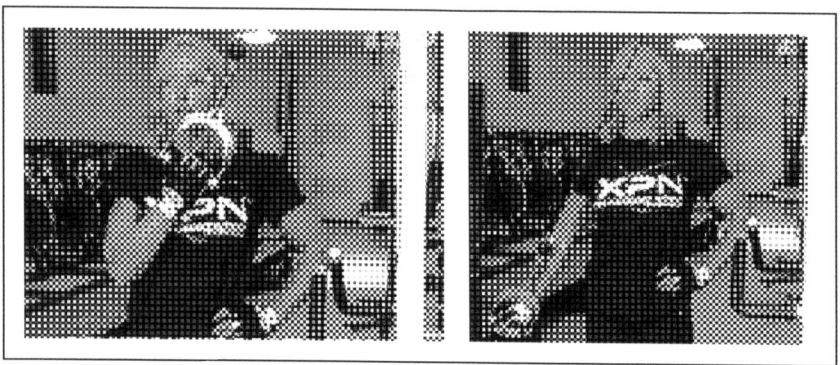

Key point(s): Keep the torsi properly aligned during the whole movement. Try to stretch the triceps at the beginning of the movement.

Deltoids activation and potentiation exercises

While the exercises used to activate the pectorals can also be used as deltoids activator, I find that deltoid activation is not necessary in most individuals as a vast majority of trainees overuse their shoulders already. I much prefer to use more metabolic work (which will be described in the next chapter) supersetted with the regular strength exercises. We can still use some potentiation exercises for the shoulders. The following movements are adequate for that purpose.

Exercise 70. Dumbbell swing

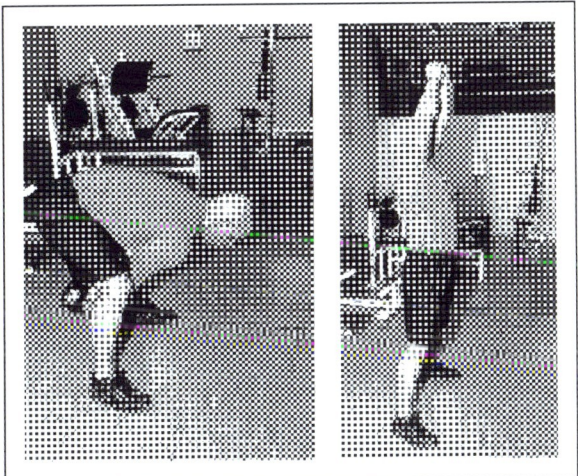

Key point(s): This exercise can also be used to potentiate the hamstrings and lower back; but if emphasis is placed on performing an explosive movement with the arms then the shoulders will play the biggest role in the exercise.

Exercise 71. 1-arm dumbbell swing

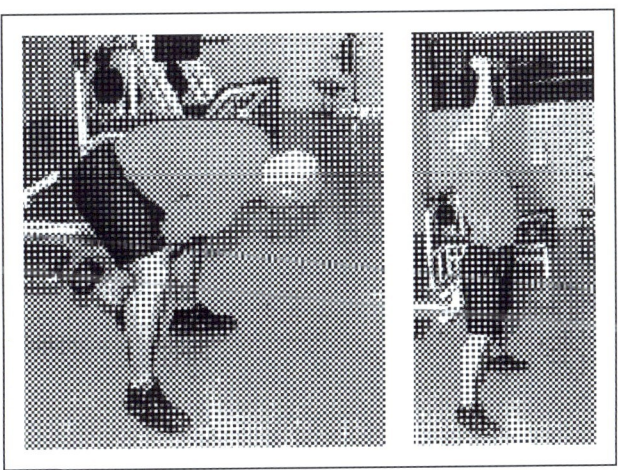

Key point(s): For both of the last two exercises, speed and explosion are key. Not just lifting the weight from point A to point B.

Exercise 72. Push press

Key point(s): This exercise, if performed with a heavy weight, can become a very good stimulation exercise. However for potentiation purposes we want to utilize a moderate weight lifted with a lot of speed and power. Use a slight push of the legs to start the bar off of the clavicle and press it explosively with the arms/shoulders.

Deltoids stimulation exercises

The deltoids are very often improperly trained either because of a bad choice of exercises or an incorrect technical application. Always remember that to be maximally effective an exercise should include: a controlled eccentric phase, a quick loaded stretch and an explosive (or an attempt to be explosive) concentric action. These things often take the wayside when we're training shoulders. Take lateral raises for example; most peoples will pause at the bottom of the movement, negating the potentiating effect of the stretch on motor unit recruitment. Others will lower the weight too rapidly (no control during the eccentric phase). These two mistakes really chip away from the effectiveness of the raises exercises (lateral, bent over, front raises). Then there is the matter of the lifting pattern. To make things simple remember this: the back end of the dumbbell should be in line or higher than the front end when you want to place more stress on the lateral head of the deltoid; the front end of the dumbbell should be higher than the back end if you want to target the anterior deltoid.

Exercise 73. Incline lateral raise

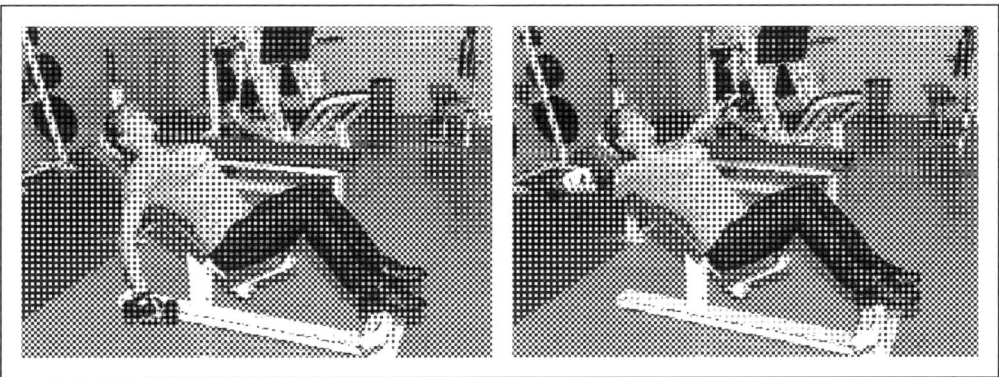

Key point(s): Because of the incline angle it is possible to get a more pronounced stretch of the deltoid by "squeezing" the arms toward the bench on the way down. Stretch those shoulders by bringing the arms back and toward the midline of the bench. Keep the back end of the dumbbell in line with the front end at the top position.

Exercise 74. Incline front raise

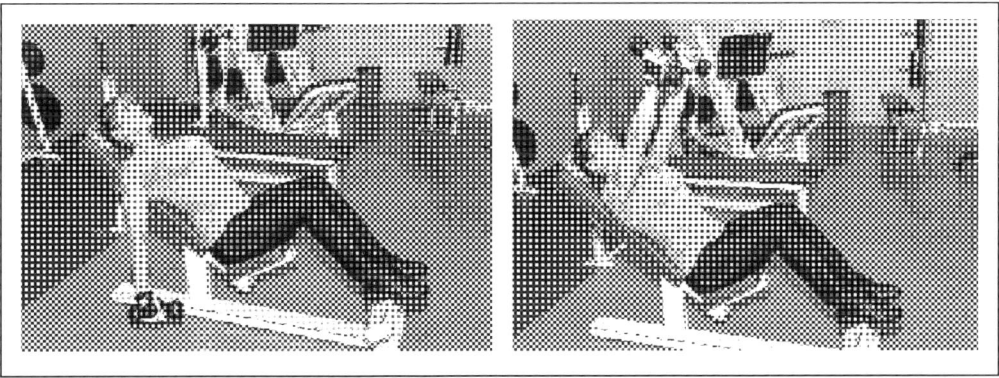

Key point(s): Stretch the front portion of the shoulder by bringing the arms far back (no need to bring them inwards) and by puffing the chest out. Lift the dumbbells with the thumbs toward the ceiling.

Exercise 75. Behind the back cable lateral raise

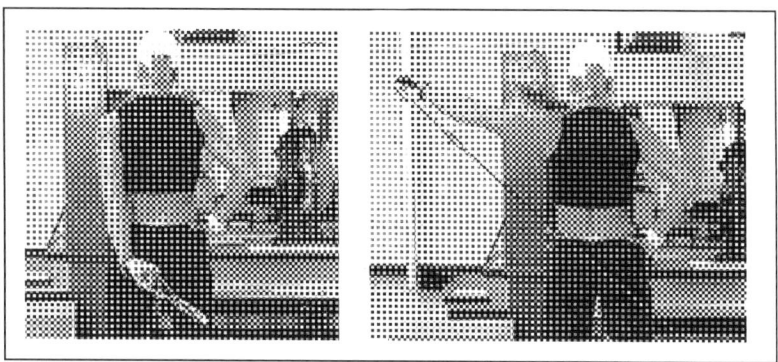

Key point(s): Stretch those shoulders by bringing the arms back and toward the midline of the body. Keep the back end of the hand in line or higher than the front end at the top position. Those with a lack of shoulder mobility can use the "in front of the body" variation, although it's a little less effective due to the decreased stretch.

Exercise 76. Behind the back cable front raise

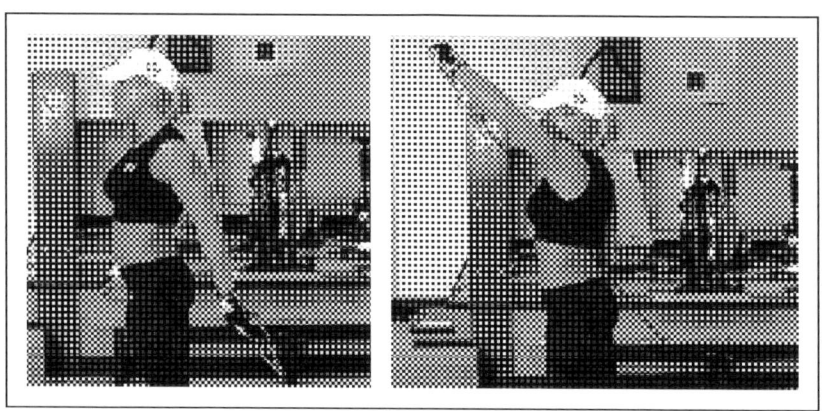

Key point(s): Stretch the front portion of the shoulder by bringing the arms far back (no need to bring them inwards) and by puffing the chest out.

Exercise 77. Arc dumbbell shoulder press

Key point(s): This is a regular shoulder press with a slight modification: at the bottom position, squeeze the elbows close to the body to stretch the shoulders. As you press the dumbbells up, do so in an arc, starting from the tucked position, pressing slightly outward at the beginning of the movement then back to inwards at the top. Bring the dumbbells close together, but don't hit them together. This exercise can also be performed seated.

Exercise 79. Barbell thrust

Key point(s): Place one end of an Olympic bar in a corner of the room and load up the weight on the other end. Bring the bar to your shoulder holding it with one hand, this is the starting position. Press it explosively while keeping the torso stable and solid. Just like with the preceding exercise, tuck the elbow close to your body to stretch the shoulder.

Exercise 80. Barbell thrust around the world

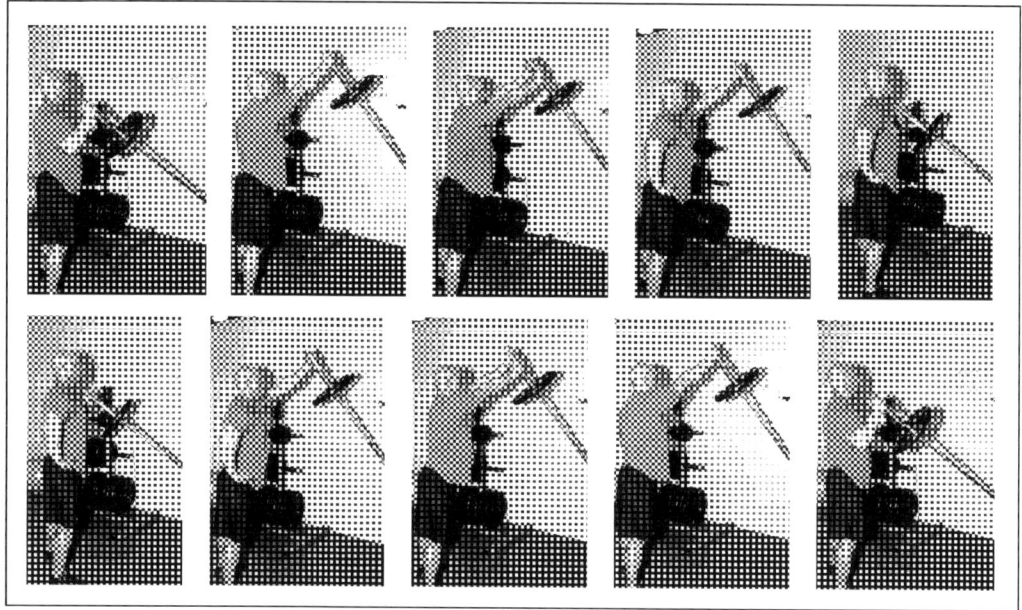

Key point(s): Place one end of an Olympic bar in a corner of the room and load up the weight on the other end. Bring the bar to your shoulder holding it with one hand, this is the starting position. Press it forward and up over your head. Exchange hands at the top position and return the bar to the starting position for the other arm. Execute the same movement from the other side. This is one complete rep.

Note: Both shoulder thrust exercises can also be performed as a push press, using a slight leg drive to get the bar moving.

Exercise 81. Behind the back two arms cross lateral raise

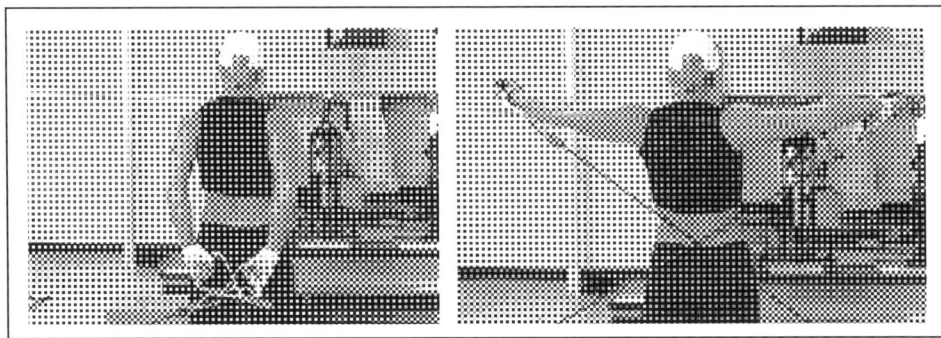

Key point(s): Stretch those shoulders by bringing the arms back and toward the midline of the body. Keep the back end of the hand in line or higher than the front end at the top position. Those with a lack of shoulder mobility can use the "in front of the body" variation, although it's a little less effective due to the decreased stretch.

Other acceptable deltoid exercises

The preceding movements can be considered to be the most efficient shoulder-builders out there. However one doesn't have to limit himself to these exercises alone. Several other movements can be very effective too.

Exercise 82. Military press

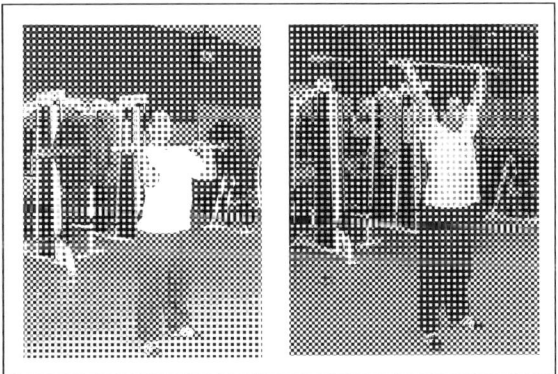

Key point(s): The military press remains a very effective deltoid exercise. The only reasons why it is not included in the "most effective list" are that tension is removed from the muscles (unloading) at the beginning of the concentric phase (because the bar rests on the clavicle) which is less effective than a loaded stretch position to recruit high-threshold motor units. This problem can be solved by not lowering the bar all the way down (bringing it down to chin level) but that will reduce the muscle stretch. Also note that the barbell doesn't allow for a movement pattern in an arc pattern like with dumbbells.

Exercise 83. Behind the neck press

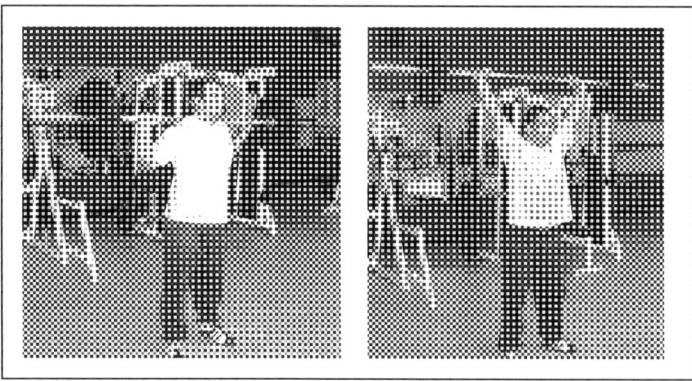

Key point(s): This movement is actually more effective than the military press when it comes to recruiting HTMUs because putting the bar behind your neck increases shoulder stretch. However the muscle unloading issue is still present. We can remedy the unloading issue by not putting the bar on the shoulders in the low position (only lowering it to ear level) but this will then reduce the deltoid stretch. This exercise is a bit more dangerous than the other shoulder movements.

Exercise 84. Seated or standing lateral raise

Key point(s): The standing and seated variations of the lateral raise are slightly less effective than the incline version because you cannot get as important of a stretch at the low position. But when properly executed (back end of the dumbbell higher, no cheating) this exercise can be effective.

Exercise 85. Gironda dumbbell swing

Key point(s): This exercise really doesn't answer the stretch demand of the hypertrophy stimulation process, but as a constant-tension exercise it can be a good addition to a shoulder program, as an assistance movement. The important point is to make the movement continuous: immediately as you reach the contracted position from one side (e.g. picture no.2) you initiate the swing to the other side, no stopping at the top or bottom positions.

Exercise 86. Standing dumbbell external rotation

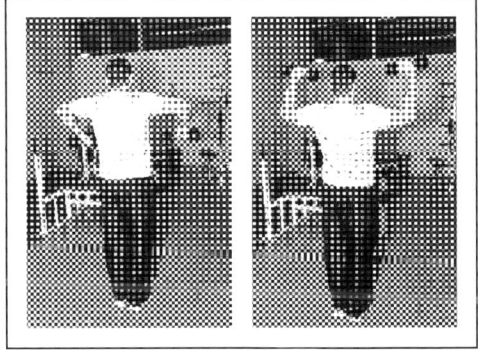

Key point(s): While this is typically a rotator cuff exercise, it can also have a good effect on all three portions of the deltoid provided that the individual tries to stretch the deltoids in the low position by rotating these shoulders as much as possible.

Hamstrings and glutes activation exercises

I prefer to see the hamstrings and glutes as one complex: the hip extensors. The following activation exercises will, however, each focus on one of these muscle groups more so than the other. While the importance of the hamstrings is fairly well known, either in the world of athletics or aesthetics, the glutes' importance isn't as well understood. However, inefficient gluteal activation (very frequent, especially in individuals with strong or tight lower back muscles) is a real problem and can lead to "gluteal amnesia" (inefficient recruitment of the glutes) which will cause a lack of trunk stability, loss of potential running speed and agility, lower back problems and glutes atrophy/sagging. By properly using glute activation exercises we can re-learn to properly activate the glutes, solving all of these potential problems.

Exercise 87. Jumpstretch bands X-walk (glutes activation)

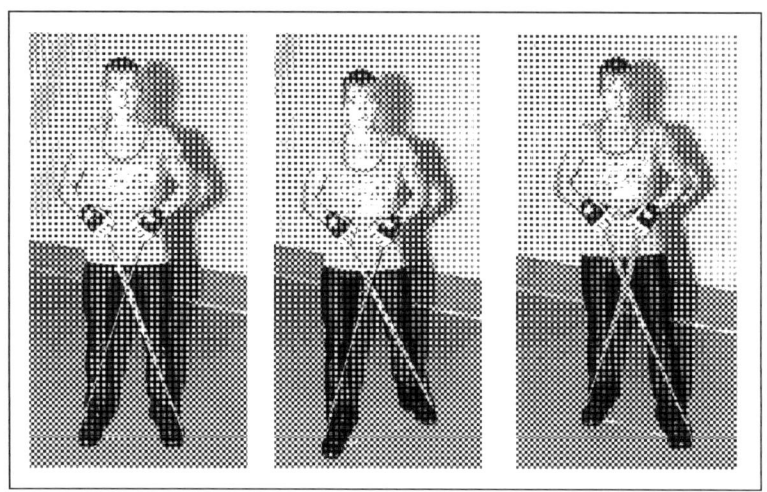

Key point(s): I learned this exercise from top performance coach Mike Boyle. You'll need a mini jumpstretch band (can be bought at www.elitefts.com). Position the band as illustrated in picture 1. For the exercise you will walk by attempting to push the hips out against the band while keeping the torso perfectly stable. Only the legs should move, not the upper body. The movement can be performed walking forward, backwards or both. Keep the shoulders down and back.

Exercise 88. Swiss ball hip extension (glutes activation)

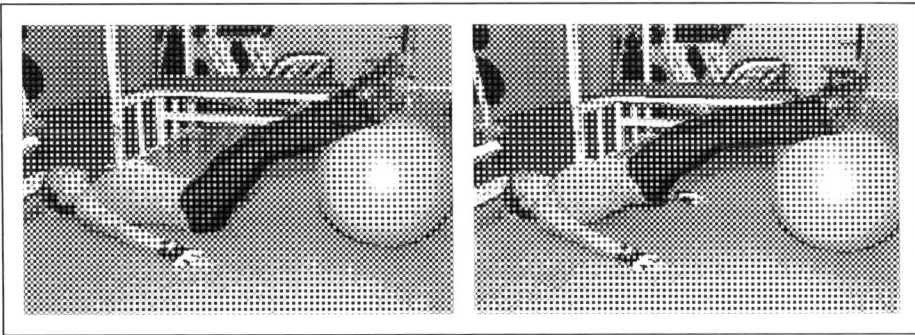

Key point(s): Lift your hips up high by focusing on flexing only the glutes. Avoid tightening the lower back at all cost. Some hamstrings activation will also happen, but really focus on squeezing those glutes hard.

Exercise 89. Swiss ball bridge (glutes activation)

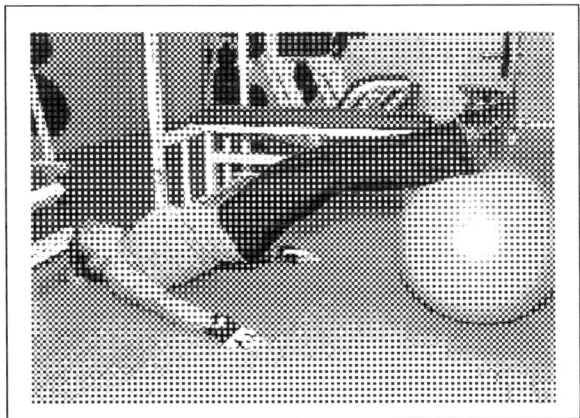

Key point(s): Same key points as above, but instead of going up and down, you hold the top position for 30-45 seconds while focusing on keeping the hips high by tensing the glutes.

Exercise 90. Swiss ball leg curl (hamstrings activation)

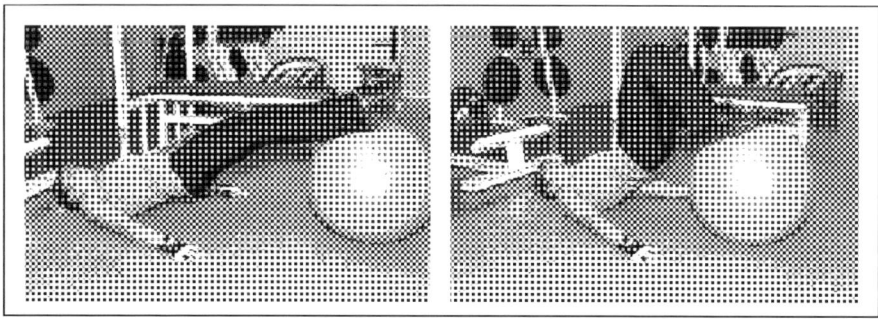

Key point(s): From the bridge position, bring the legs toward your body by flexing the hamstring muscles. As an advanced variation, this movement can be performed with only one leg on the ball.

Exercise 91. Cook lift (glutes activation and testing)

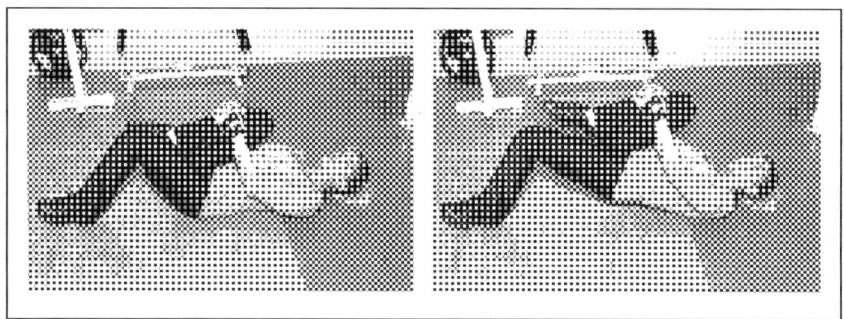

Key point(s): Bend the working leg at 90 degrees. Put only the heel on the ground. Bring the other leg towards your chest and hold it there. From that position lift your hips up using only the glute. If you feel it in your hamstrings it means that your gluteal recruitment pattern is faulty (and you'll need to perform more glute activation drills). If you feel it only in your glutes, you can use this exercise as an activation exercise by performing sets of 4-6 reps per leg, holding the top position for 5 seconds per rep. If you feel it only in your hamstrings, you are better off using other glutes activation movements first.

Hamstrings and glutes potentiation exercises

For both of these muscle groups the Olympic lift variations and dumbbell swing exercises (described in the deltoid potentiation section) are good movements to use. Variations of the jump lunges and jump step-ups can also be used.

Exercise 92. Split squat jump

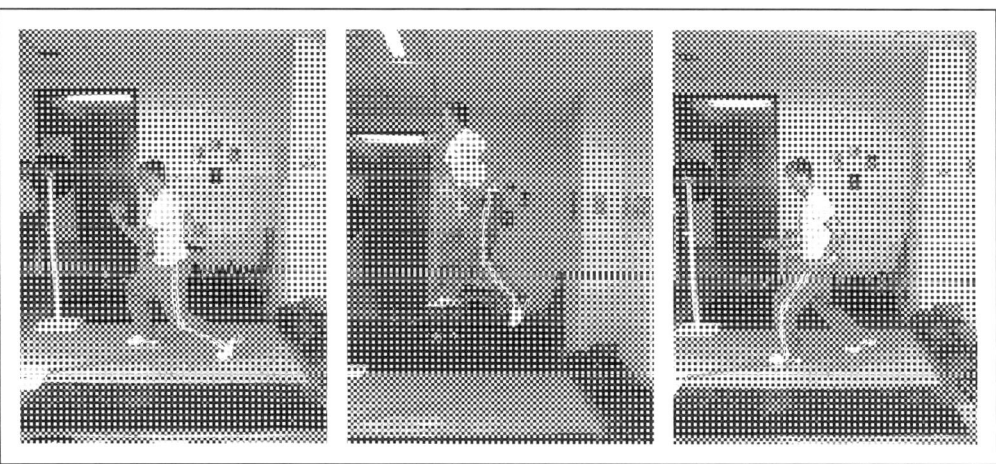

Key point(s): A wider stance will focus more on the hamstrings while a closer stance will involve the glutes and quads more. Switch legs in the air and jump back up as soon as you land.

Exercise 93. Loaded split squat jump

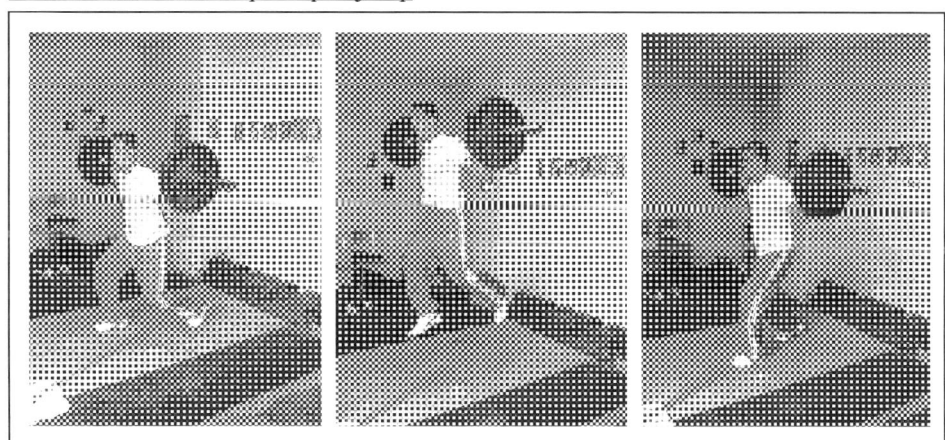

Key point(s): A wider stance will focus more on the hamstrings while a closer stance will involve the glutes and quads more. Switch legs in the air and jump back up as soon as you land. Limit yourself to using around 10-15% of your max squat for this exercise.

Exercise 94. Step-up jump

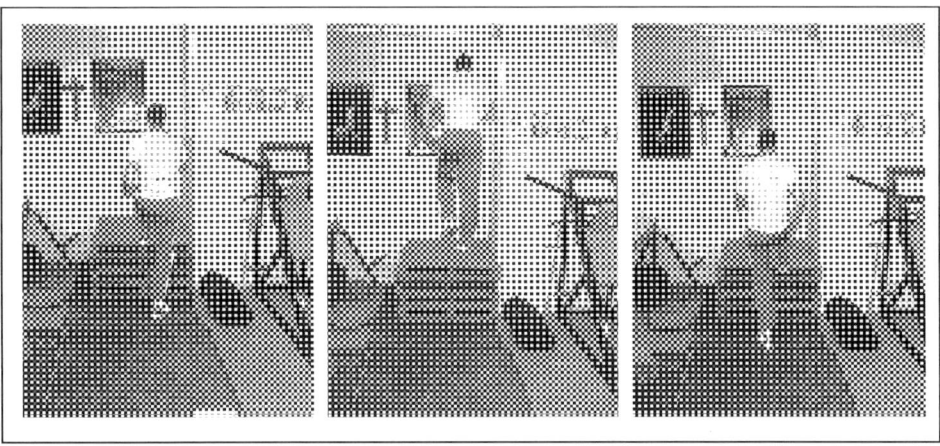

Key point(s): Focus on jumping only by pushing with the elevated leg. The higher the box/step is, the more hamstrings come into play. Switch legs in the air. As you jump, do not use your back to project yourself up, focus on pushing with your glute.

Hamstrings and glutes stimulation exercises
Stimulating the hamstrings is a little like doing so for the biceps: it's impossible to stretch that muscle by performing a single joint movement. As a result, leg curl variations will always be inferior to exercises such as the Romanian deadlift, stiff-leg deadlift, Goodmorning and long step lunges. In fact, for athletic training the leg curl is a superfluous exercise. It can have its place in a muscle-building program though, but not as a prime exercise.

Exercise 95. Long step lunges

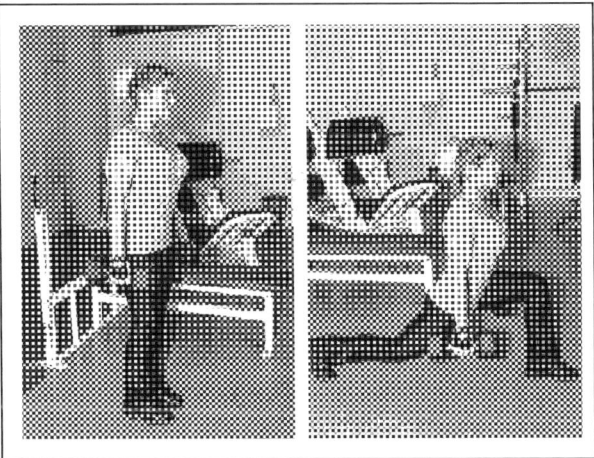

Key point(s): The wide step involves the hamstring a little more. Always keep the torso solid and upright. Bring the knee of the back leg as close to the floor as possible without touching it.

Exercise 96. Medium step lunges

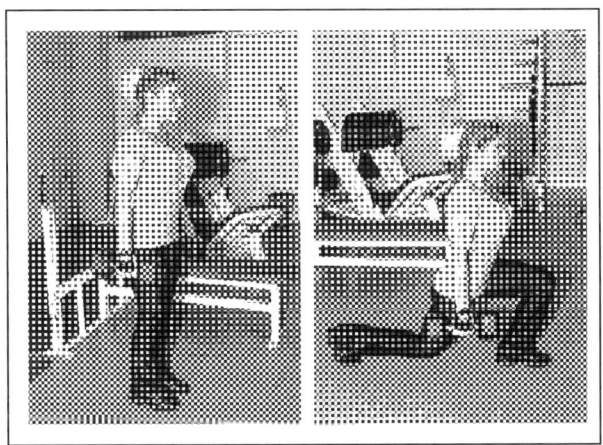

Key point(s): The medium step involves the glutes a little more. Always keep the torso solid and upright. Bring the knee of the back leg as close to the floor as possible without touching it.

Exercise 97. Romanian deadlift

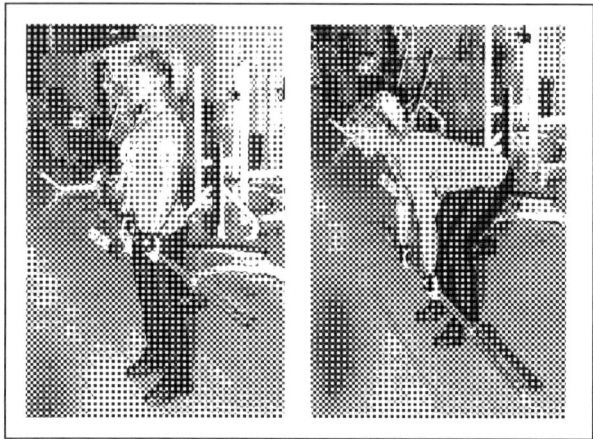

Key point(s): Keep the knees bent at around a 135 degrees angle. Lower the bar by pushing your hips back. Keep the lower back flat. Focus on getting a good stretch in the hamstrings

Exercise 98. Dumbbell Romanian deadlift

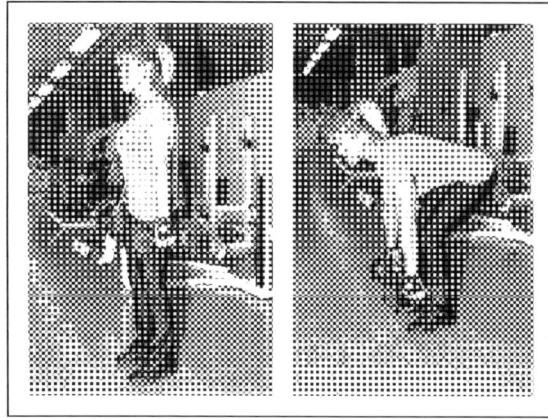

Key point(s): Keep the knees bent at around a 135 degrees angle. Lower the bar by pushing your hips back. Keep the lower back flat. Focus on getting a good stretch in the hamstrings. The advantage of the dumbbell variation is that you don't have to have an internally rotated shoulder position as you do with the barbell. The arms can stay in a more natural position.

Exercise 99. Stiff-leg deadlift

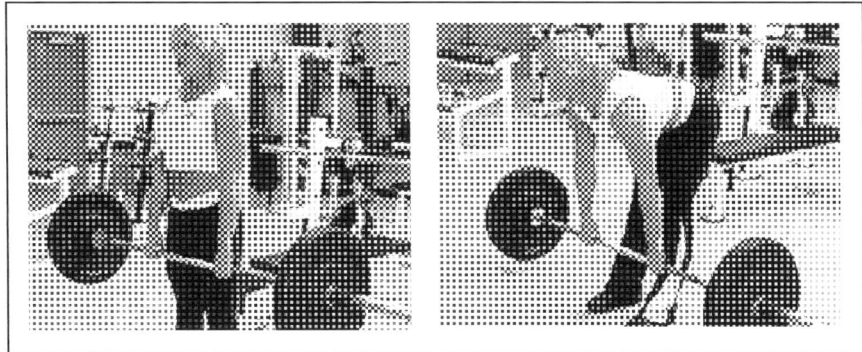

Key point(s): Keep the legs straight. Lower the bar by pushing your hips back. Keep the lower back flat. Focus on getting a good stretch in the hamstrings.

Exercise 100. Leg press high feet

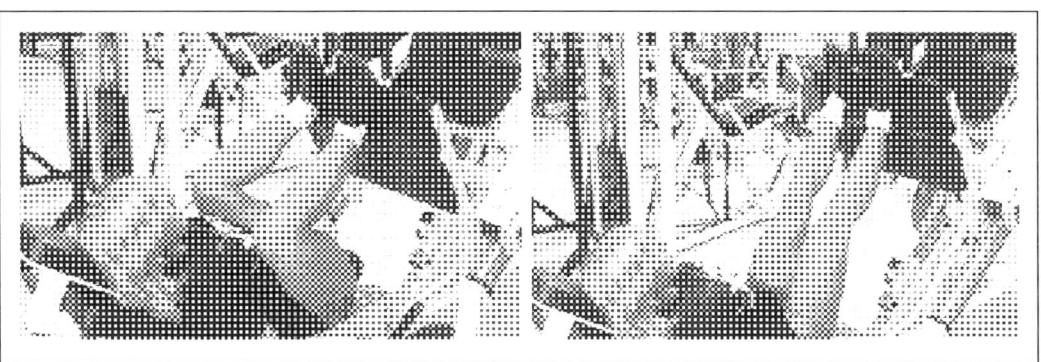

Key point(s): Only the heels should be on the pad; curl up your toes to shift the weight toward the heels.

Exercise 101. Reverse hyper on back extension station

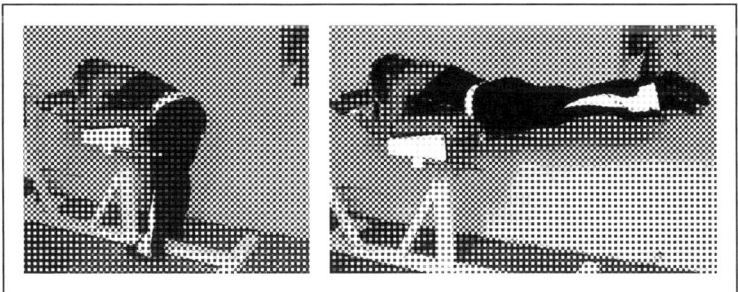

Key point(s): Obviously this exercise is best performed on a "real" reverse hyper station, but very few gyms actually have one. It is possible to use the back extension bench to perform this drill. If you need to add weight you can attach a dumbbell between your feet with a lifting belt or use ankle weights. Keep the legs straight and stretch those hamstrings at the bottom position.

Exercise 102. Side hip extension

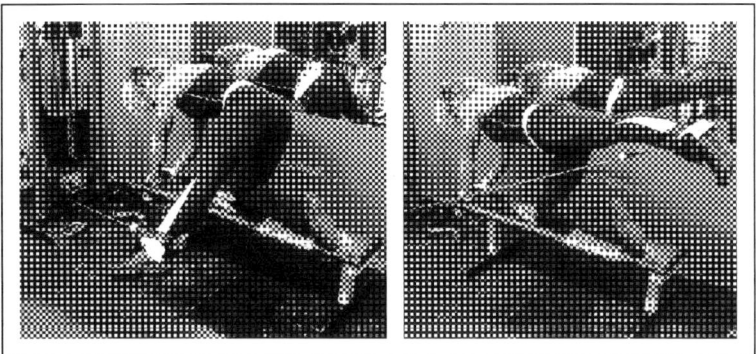

Key point(s): Bring the leg forward and to the side in the starting position, to get a better stretch. Then push it back and inwards while keeping the leg straight. Focus on tensing the glutes during the movement.

Exercise 103. Backward kick

Key point(s): Bring the knee forward to stretch the glute in the starting position. Extend the hip back. Focus on activating the glutes, not the lower back.

Other decent hamstrings exercises

The following exercises are not as functional as the preceding ones and are somewhat inferior for an overall hypertrophic effect due to the absence of a maximal strength. However for someone training only to improve looks and gain muscle, these exercises can be a good addition to a training program.

Exercise 104. Gironda leg curl

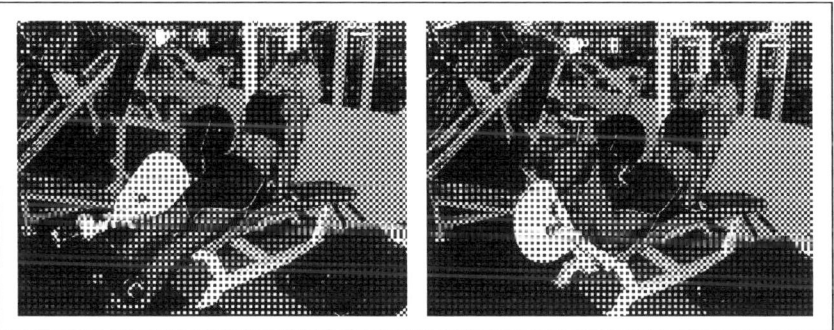

Key point(s): Perform a regular leg curl but with an elevated torso. The arms are extended to keep the upper body high but the legs stay in the bench.

Exercise 105. Standing leg curl

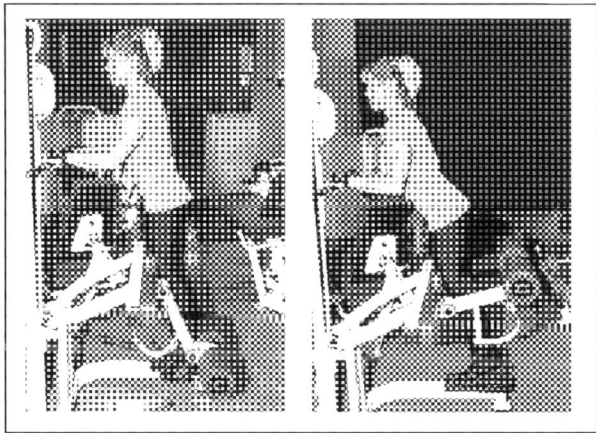

Key point(s): This is a pretty straight-forward exercise, not real need to describe it!

Exercise 106. 1-leg curl

Key point(s): Like with most machine exercises, I prefer to use the unilateral version of the movement to at least get some added HTMU recruitment which will make these exercises more effective.

Exercise 107. Lying leg curl

Key point(s): This is a pretty straight-forward exercise, not real need to describe it!

Note: With all leg curl exercises you can change the feet position to alter muscle recruitment somewhat. When the feet are turned out you will put more stress on the outer portion of the hamstrings complex (both sections of the biceps femoris), when the feet are turned in you will put more stress on the medial portion of the hamstrings complex (semitendinosus and semimembranosus). A neutral feet position will active pretty much all portions equally.

Quadriceps activation exercises

When we're talking about quadriceps activation we refer mostly to the vastus medialis (tear drop-shaped muscle next you're your knee) because this muscle is an active stabilizer of the knee joint. A lot of peoples, especially women have problems recruiting and activating the VMO and as a result they tend to rely excessively on the vastus lateralis muscle (outer portion of the quads). This will cause a muscle imbalance that could very well result in a knee injury. In that regard quadriceps or VMO activation drills can be very important to some individuals. Remember that to be effective the source of instability (if instability is used to increase quadriceps activation) must be beneath the working leg(s). If you perform a split squat with the back leg on a swiss ball, it will not be as effective as if you were doing a split squat with the front leg on an unstable surface: the closer to the source of instability a muscle is, the more it will be affected by the exercise.

Exercise 108. Squat feet on foam/airex pads

Key point(s): The foam pad provides a small instability that isn't exceedingly hard to master. It's just enough to increase muscle activation without changing the biodynamics of the movement. Do not wear your shoes when you perform this exercise: performing this exercise barefoot (or with socks) will allow for a better activation of the baroreceptors of the feet which will enhance quadriceps activity.

Exercise 109. Split squat feet on foam/airex pads

Key point(s): Prevent the knees from buckling in. Contrary to popular belief, it's perfectly okay to let the knee travel past the toes. In fact this prestretch the quadriceps more, leading to a greater activation. In the illustration Christiane is performing an advanced version of the movement by keeping the heels off of the pads.

Exercise 110. Lunges feet on foam/airex pads

Key point(s): This movement is similar to the preceding one, except that you start with only on foot on a pad, the other one is in the air then you land it on the second pad.

Exercise 111. "Siffie" split squat and "Siffie" lunges

Key point(s): This method comes from the great sport scientist Mel Siff Ph.D. In consists of reducing the support base by performing the exercise on your toes. This creates a certain instability and forces a greater quadriceps activation. Stay on your toes for the duration of the set. When you perform the lunge variation the dynamic action of the body increases the stabilization demand and thus the activation of the quadriceps.

Quadriceps potentiation exercises

To potentiate the quadriceps we can use any type of jumping exercise as well as explosive lifts such as jump squats and speed squats. The key is that explosive movements wake-up the nervous system and improves your capacity to recruit the muscle.

Soviet Olympic lifters used to perform a maximal vertical jump at the beginning of their training sessions and before a competition lift for that specific purpose. Powerlifting legend Fred Hatfield Ph.D. also did the same thing prior to a max squat attempt.

Exercise 112. Sit jumps

Key point(s): Sit on a box or bench so that your legs are bent at close to a 90 degrees angle. Jump back onto the box utilizing as little back movement as possible: focus on jumping only with your quads. Since the landing surface is higher than the jumping surface, the shock on the joints and tendons is minimal.

Exercise 113. Box jumps

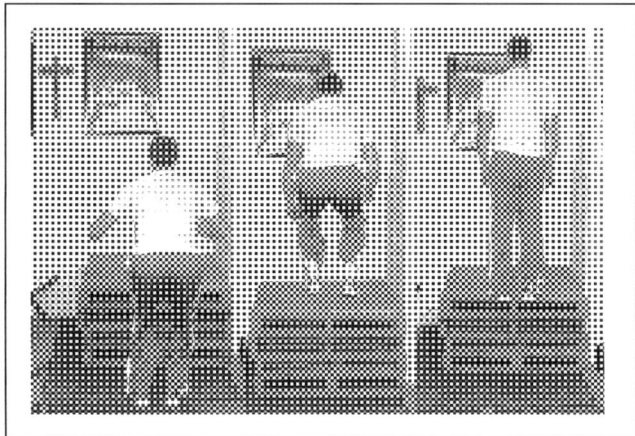

Key point(s): Jump onto the box from the ground. Since the landing surface is higher than the jumping surface, the shock on the joints and tendons is minimal.

Exercise 114. Step-up jumps

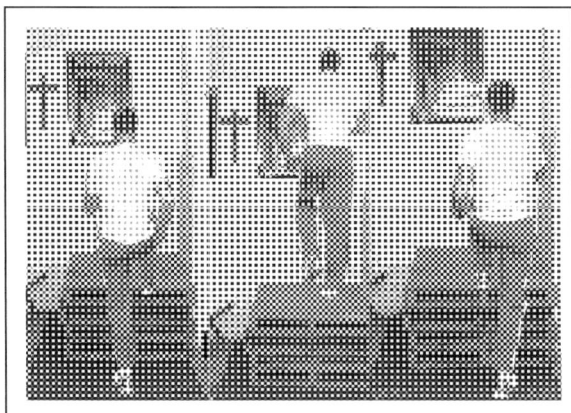

Key point(s): Jump up using only the leg that is on the box. Focus on getting a full extension of that leg. Switch side in the air.

Exercise 115. Jump squat

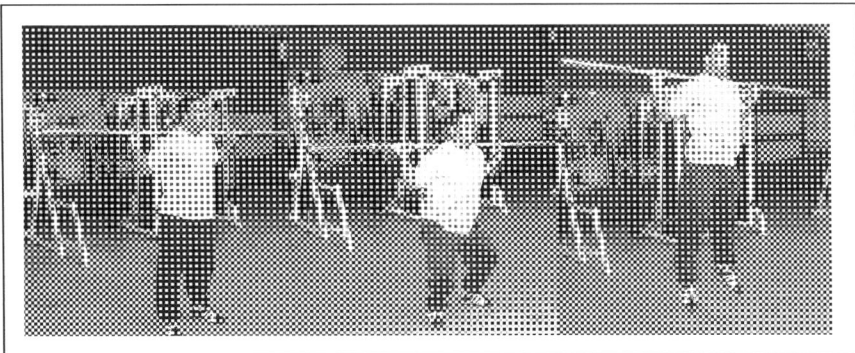

Key point(s): Bend the knees only as far down as you would for a vertical jump. Immediately as you reach the low position jump up as high as you can. Upon landing, resent yourself properly and begin each repetition from the starting position. Use a load that is between 10 and 20% of your maximum squat weight.

Exercise 116. Jump squat series

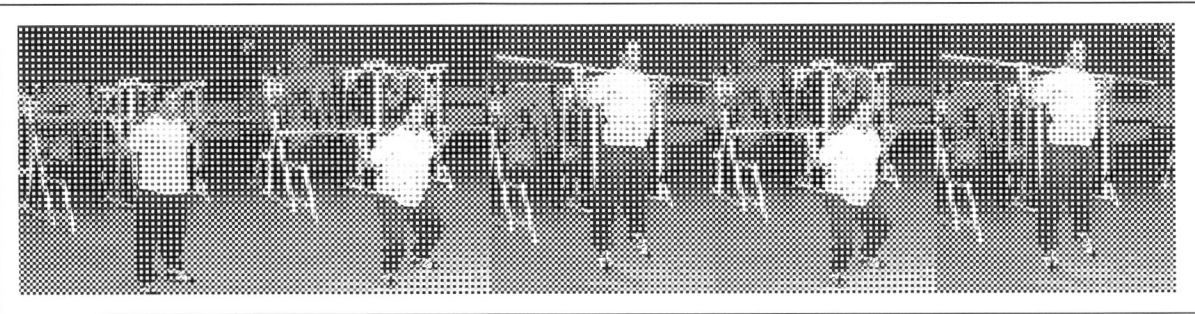

Key point(s): This is similar to the preceding exercise except that you don't reset between reps: immediately as you land on the floor you jump back up in the air.

Exercise 117. Iso-dynamic jump squat

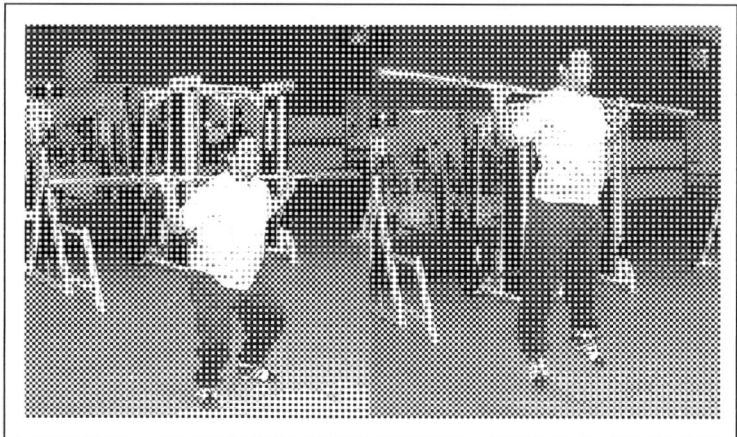

Key point(s): For this variation of the exercise you start each repetition from a static bent-knee position. You hold there for 2-3 seconds before jumping up in the air. This pause will negate the participation of the strength reflex so you will have to rely mostly on muscle power to project yourself. For athletes this variation is better to develop the capacity to explode from a static start (football lineman or sprinter out of the blocks) while the preceding one is better to increase speed by improving both the muscle and reflex/elastic aspects of force production.

Quadriceps stimulation exercises

When it comes to stimulating the quadriceps the key is "full range of motion". As we saw earlier, reaching a stretched position is an effective way of increasing muscle recruitment. So when you are performing a squat, if you stop at the quarter squat position you will not optimally recruit the quadriceps. If you have flexibility issues that prevent you from performing full range-of-motion squats, then you should use other exercises such as split squats and lunges until you resolve your flexibility problem.

Exercise 118. Front squat

Key point(s): When it comes to building the quadriceps I prefer the front squat over the back squat because it's much harder to compensate with the lower back (you have to maintain an upright position or drop the bar) and as a result more stress is placed on the quads. If you lack the flexibility to use a clean grip, you can use a crossed-arm grip (illustrated at the right).

Christiane in the middle of a set of front squats

Exercise 119. Back squat

Key point(s): To maximize quadriceps stimulation you must use a moderate width (or even narrow) stance and keep the torso upright as much as possible to unload the lower back.

Exercise 120. Belt squat

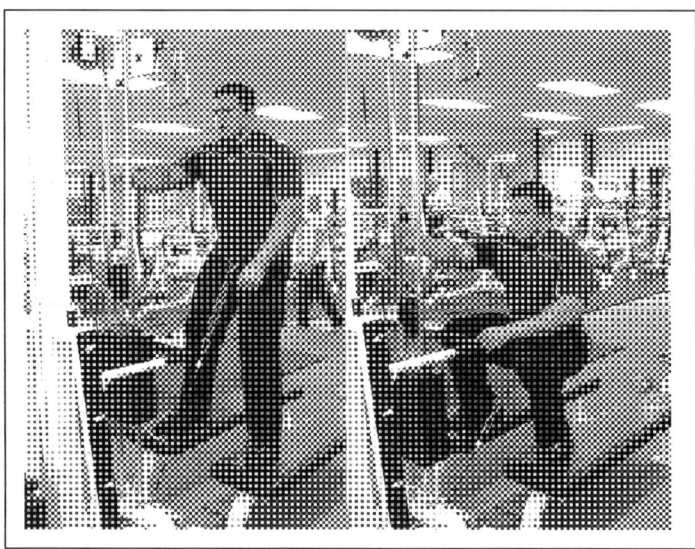

Key point(s): The cable pulls you forward and thus allows you to lean back more as you squat, so you can get a better quadriceps stretch. The movement also unloads the back so the quads take on the bulk of the work.

Exercise 121. Close stance hack squat

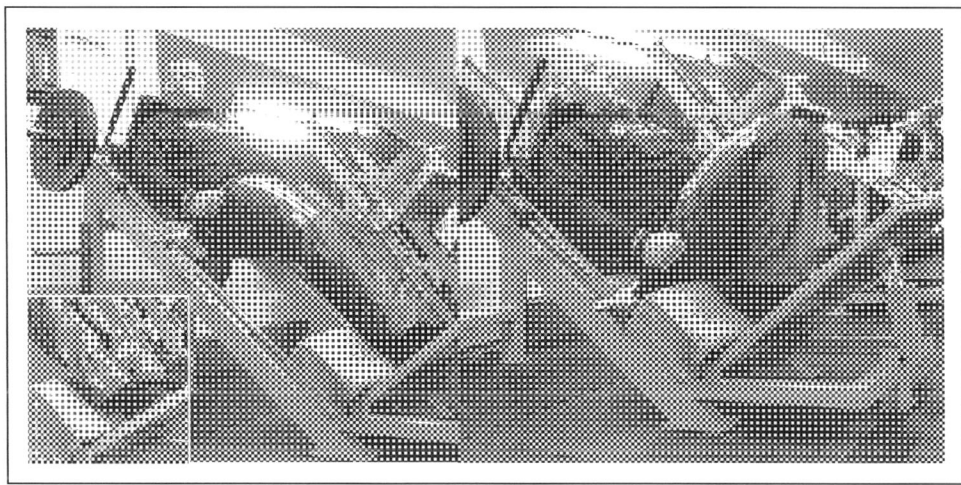

Key point(s): Keep the legs in contact with each other for the duration of the movement. Elevate the heels to allow for a better quadriceps stretch and a decreased glutes activation.

Exercise 122. Frog stance hack squat

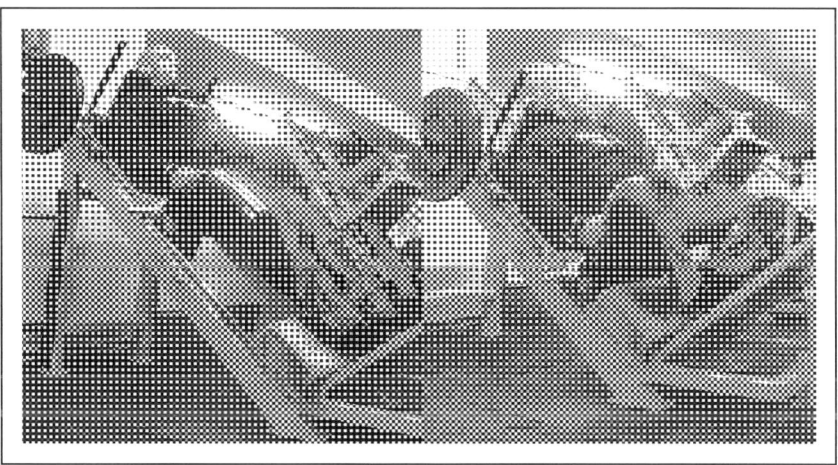

Key point(s): Push the knees out on the way down and bring them back in during the lifting action. Keep your heels elevated to decrease glutes activation.

Exercise 123. Sissy squat

Key point(s): Keep your heels elevated and your hips up high for the duration of the movement; don't let them drop down.

Exercise 124. Short step lunges

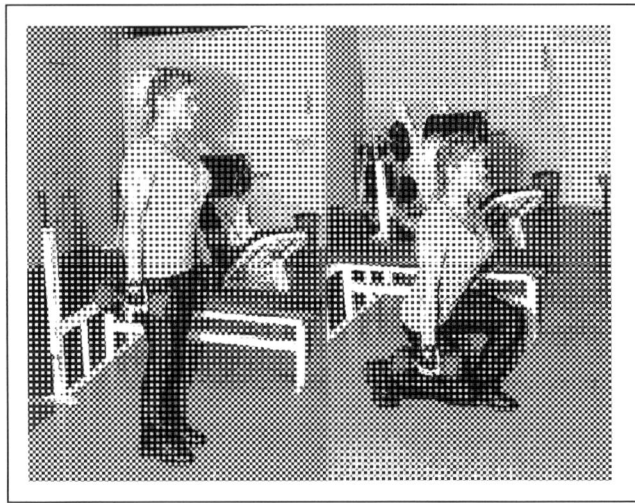

Key point(s): Keep the chest puffed out and the torso solid. The back knee should come close to the floor, but not touch it.

Exercise 125. Bulgarian split squat

Key point(s): Keep the torso upright and bring the back knee as close to the floor as possible, without actually touching it. This movement can also be done with dumbbells.

Exercise 126. Front elevated lunge

Key point(s): Performing this exercise with the front foot lading on a block increases the overall lower body stretch and makes this exercise all the more effective. It can also be done using dumbbells.

Exercise 127. Dumbbell squat

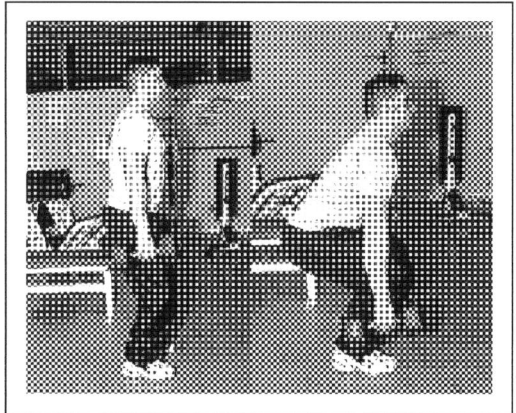

Key point(s): Stop just short of the lockout to maintain quadriceps tension during the whole exercise. Use a narrow stance.

Other decent quadriceps exercises

The following movements can be added to your program; however they should only be used as secondary exercises. They are effective, but they are not the MOST effective drills for the quadriceps.

Exercise 128. Leg press

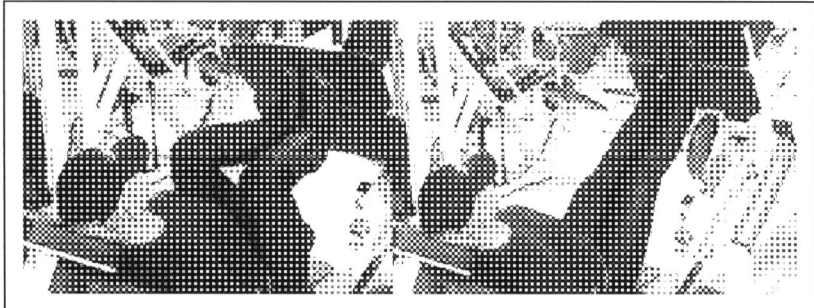

Key point(s): While you should use a full range of motion at the knees, you shouldn't go so low that your tailbone or lower back leaves the seat. This will place a lot of stress on the lower back. You can vary your stance to chance the portion of the quadriceps that you emphasise: the closer the stance, the more you'll stimulate the outer portion and vice-versa.

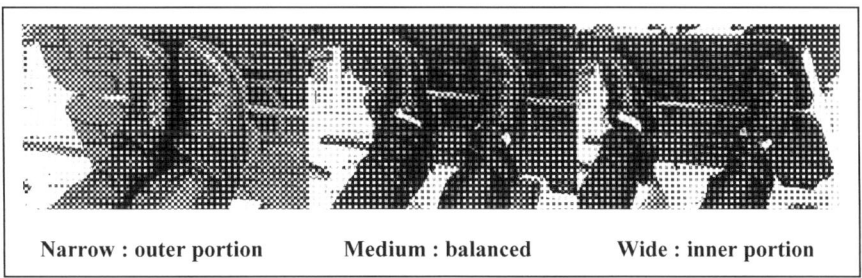

Narrow : outer portion   Medium : balanced   Wide : inner portion

Exercise 129. 1-Leg extension

Key point(s): Much like with the machine curl, I prefer the unilateral version of this exercise for its greater capacity to activate HTMUs. The foot angle can also be changed to vary the muscle activation pattern: turn the feet out to focus more on the inner portion of the quadriceps and turn them in to put more emphasis on the outer portion.

Exercise 130. Leg extension

Key point(s): The foot angle can also be changed to vary the muscle activation pattern: turn the feet out to focus more on the inner portion of the quadriceps and turn them in to put more emphasis on the outer portion.

Abdominal activation exercises

Any exercise performed on an unstable surface (not just abdominal movements) will activate the abdominal muscles because of the increased core stability demands. So in that regard, if you train the abdominals at the end of your workout it might not be necessary to utilize an activation exercise specific to the abdominals. If you are training your abs first in a workout or on a day of their own then you might want to include specific activation movements such as swiss ball crunches, swiss ball rotations, bridges and forward rolls.

Exercise 131. Swiss ball crunch

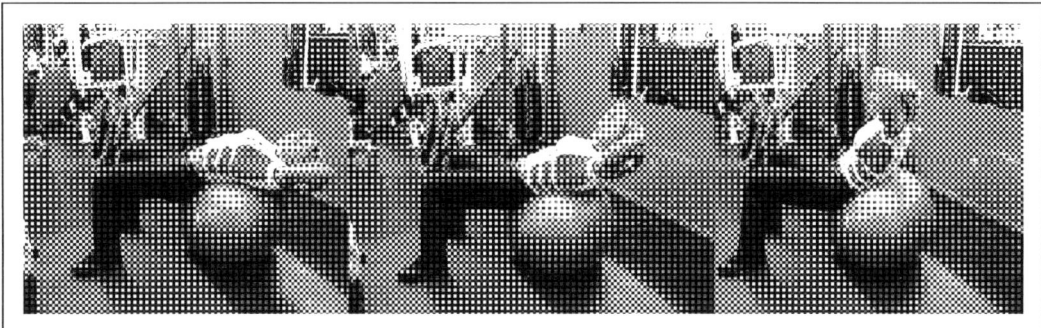

Key point(s): The crunch is not a flexion at the trunk but rather a "rolling" motion of the whole trunk. Imagine that you are trying to roll up your upper body on a cylinder lying on your abdomen. Go for a full stretch position on every repetition.

Exercise 132. Pulldown swiss ball crunch

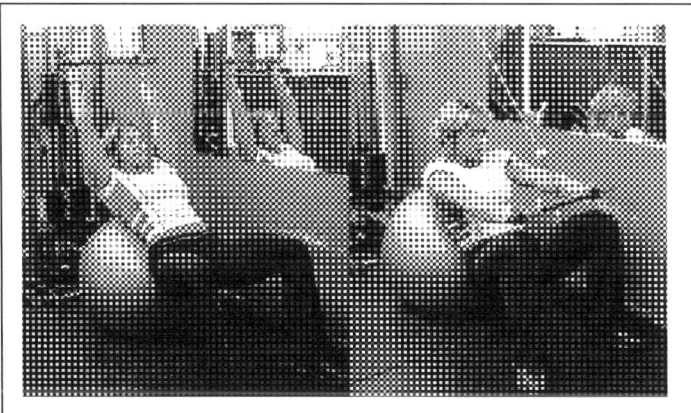

Key point(s): Stretch the arm above the head in the starting position; as you crunch, pulldown the bar towards your legs.

Exercise 133. Pulldown swiss ball crunch

Key point(s): Rotate the trunk from one side to the other while keeping the trunk in a crunch position. Do no rotate the hips, only the trunk/torso.

Abdominal stimulation exercises

Here are what I consider to be the best exercises for the abdominals. When training abs I normally use:

a) Post-fatigue supersets with the first exercise being a loaded (with added resistance) movement and the second one being an unloaded (no added weight) drill working the same movement pattern.

b) Circuits of 4-5 exercises working all the functions of the trunk: 1) rotation 2) lateral flexion 3) trunk flexion 4) hip flexion. Below is an example of such a circuit. This is the functional circuit I used with my hockey players in 2002.

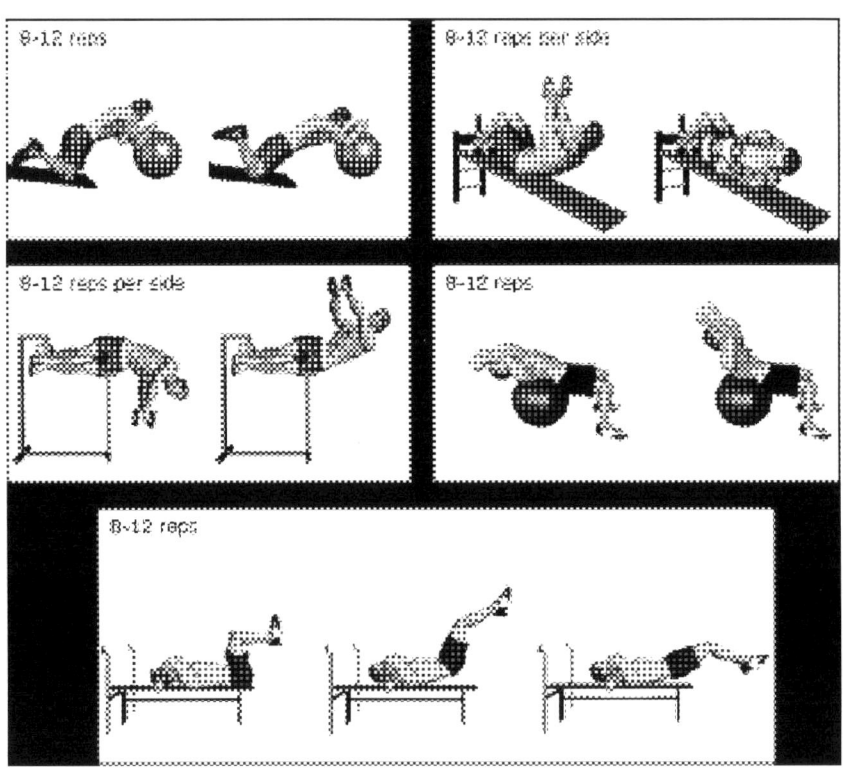

Trunk flexion exercises

Exercise 134. Kneeling cable crunch

Key point(s): As with the other crunching movements the objective is to perform a "rolling of the spine" not a mere trunk flexion. Performing the movement while kneeling reduced the activation of the hip flexors and puts more stress on the abdominal muscles.

Exercise 135. Serratus crunch

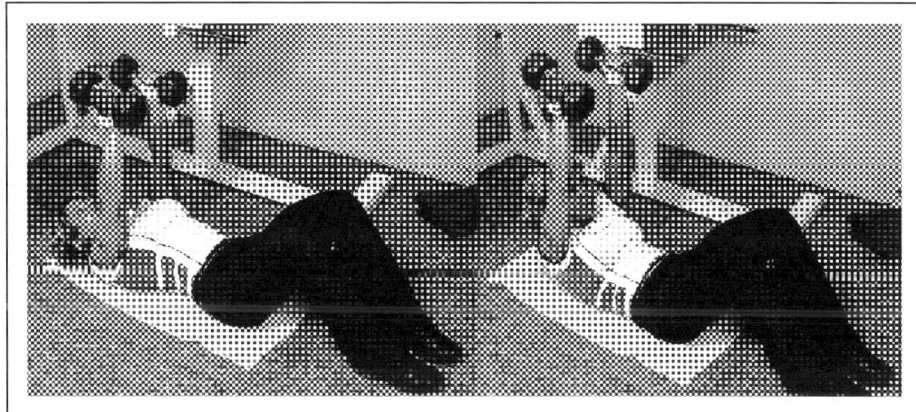

Key point(s): Keep the elbows locked throughout the whole movement. When you curl/crunch up, also push the dumbbells straight towards the ceiling to activate the serratus.

Exercise 136. Weighted crunch

Key point(s): Focus again on rolling the spine forward, not bending the trunk. The movement should always be performed under control, do not jerk yourself up.

Exercise 137. Low-pulley cable crunch

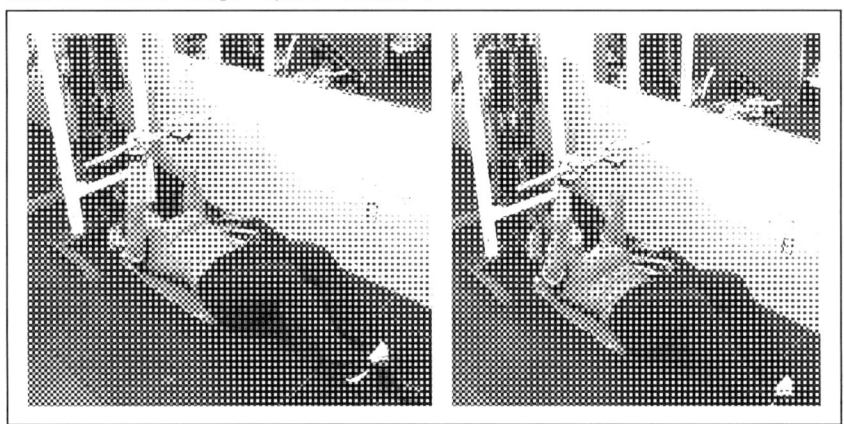

Key point(s): Bring the arms above the head in the starting position; as you crunch, push the bar towards the ceiling focusing on getting a peak contraction of the abdominal muscles.

Hip flexion movements

Exercise 138. Hanging leg raise

Key point(s): Initiate the movement by flexing the glutes in the starting position. When the glutes are activated, you can perform the leg raise portion of the movement.

Exercise 139. Hanging leg raise on Hack squat machine

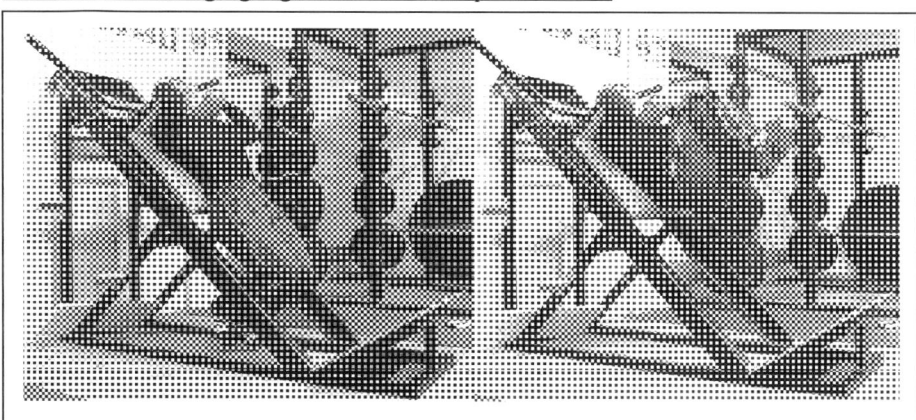

Key point(s): This variation is slightly easier than the pure hanging raise. And the back support generally facilitate the proper execution of the movement. At the top position try to "tuck in" your knees by lifting your glutes off of the back support.

Exercise 140. Double crunch exchange

Key point(s): Always keep a certain tension in your abdominals by avoiding brining either the legs or shoulders all the way back down during the movement.

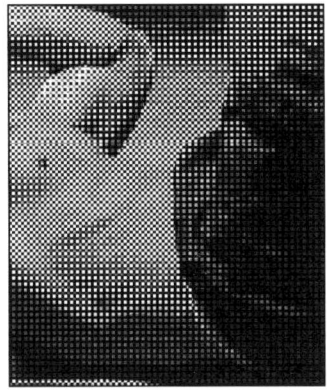

Exercise 140. Knee tuck-in

Key point(s): Always keep the tension on the abdominals by not bringing the legs all the way down and by voluntarily contracting the abs as hard as you can throughout the duration of the exercise.

Trunk rotation exercises

Exercise 141. Twisting cable crunch

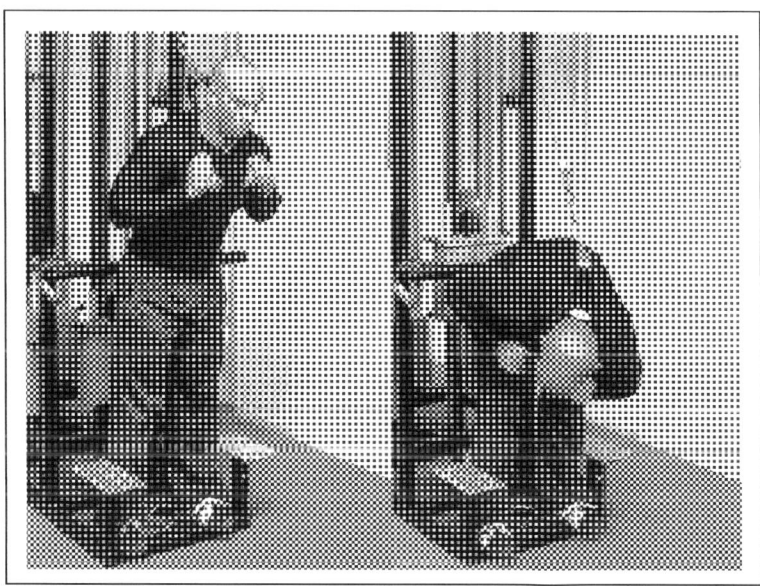

Key point(s): Can also be performed kneeling and facing the pulley station.

Exercise 142. High pulley woodchop

Key point(s): Keep the glutes tensed to stabilize the hips. Rotate with the trunk alone, not the hips. Can also be done standing, but there will be an increased tendency to rotate the hips.

Exercise 143. Low pulley woodchop

Key point(s): Same execution as the previous exercise except that you use the low pulley station instead of the high one.

Exercise 144. Full Russian Twist on Swiss ball

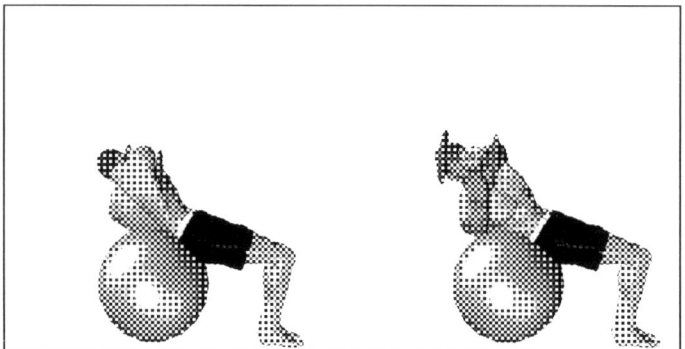

Key point(s): Rotate the trunk from one side to the other while keeping the trunk in a crunch position. Do no rotate the hips, only the trunk/torso. Keep the arms fully extended during the whole movement. Go from the fully rotated right position to the fully rotated left position and return.

Exercise 145. Half Russian Twist on Swiss ball

Key point(s): Rotate the trunk from one side to the other while keeping the trunk in a crunch position. Do no rotate the hips, only the trunk/torso. Keep the arms fully extended during the whole movement. Perform all reps from one side and then do the other side.

Exercise 146. Tornado

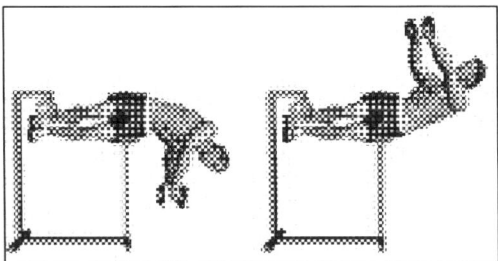

Key point(s): This is an advanced exercise that shouldn't be done by individuals who have lower back problems. If you decide to utilise this movement, always perform it slowly and under control. It combines a lateral flexion with a trunk rotation. Keep the hips fixed at all times, focusing on trunk rotation and flexion only.

Lateral flexion exercises

Exercise 147. Dumbbell side bend

Key point(s): The important thing is to keep the upper body properly aligned during the lowering phase; a lot of peoples go down not only to the side, but rotate forward as well, this is a mistake. Imagine performing this exercise back to the wall, keeping your whole back touching the wall at all times. IDIOT WATCH: Only use one dumbbell at a time. I see a lot of guys/gals performing this exercise holding one dumbbell in each end. This is stupid since the opposite dumbbell acts as a counterweight which makes the movement so much easier that it almost becomes worthless.

Exercise 148. Saxon side bend

Key point(s): Everything that applied for the preceding exercise (except for the idiot watch comment) applies for this exercise too. It can also be performed with a single dumbbell held with both hands.

Exercise 149. Low pulley side bend

Key point(s): This movement is similar to the regular side bend with the exception that you will be using a low pulley station instead of a dumbbell. Hold the handle with the right hand when working your left side and vice versa.

PRINCIPLE 10
When trying to lose fat, add high-speed metabolic work

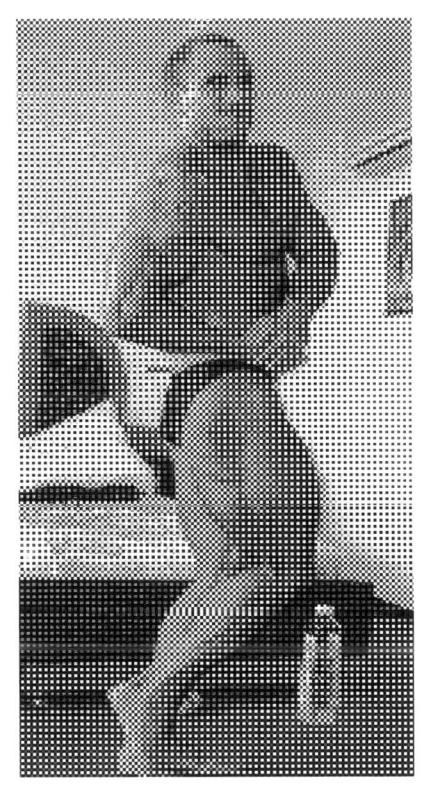

Introduction

I first discussed high-speed metabolic work in 2003 in an article I wrote for T-nation.com titled *"Superman sets"*. The basic premise of this method was, and still is, to perform as much physical work as possible during a set time frame. With this type of training very fast reps with a relatively light source of resistance (free-weight or elastic resistance) is the preferred approach. The objective is to perform as many complete reps as possible in the time frame prescribed by the program. This method fits right in with the high-threshold training mentality since explosiveness, speed and power are emphasized. Just like with the "regular" strength exercises, during superman sets/high-speed metabolic work movement speed will eventually decrease as fatigue sets in. However it is the intent to accelerate that remains paramount to the success of this method.

Why high-speed reps?

Metabolic work should emphasize speed reps because these will put more strain on the fast-twitch fibers/HTMUs. Even the recruited and stimulated mixed fibers will tend to adapt to this type of training by changing their profile towards a fast-twitch one. HTMUs also tend to rely mostly on glucose for fuel. This source of energy leads to an acidification of the blood and muscle which stimulates the release of growth hormone. As you probably know, growth hormone can both stimulate muscle growth and fat loss. While a transient hormonal stimulation isn't going to have the same effect as using exogenous chemicals, over the long-term it can play a significant role in stimulating a positive change in body composition. Simply look at the physique of athletes who compete in sports revolving around performing a lot of work in a short period of time (sprints, speed skating, jumping events, gymnastics, etc.) and you'll see that, on average, they are the leanest and most muscular group around (without even trying to get these kind of results). So when doing metabolic work in the gym, the emphasis should be on performing as many speed reps as possible within a time frame that can lead to a significant elevation in blood acidity/lactate. Also remember that moving fast burns more energy than moving slowly. Take a car engine for example: it will burn more fuel running at 7000RPM than when running at 3000RPM. So for the same time frame, fast movements will use more calories than slower ones, which is the primary objective of metabolic sets.

What set duration should we use?

When using metabolic work with muscle growth and fat loss in mind the set duration should allow for the use of a moderate weigh, lifted at high speed and while inducing an increase in lactate production. Sets of less than 20 seconds should be ruled out because these will rely mostly on the phosphagen energy system (ATP and creatine phosphate) which doesn't lead to a significant elevation of blood lactate. Sets lasting longer than 60 seconds should also be ruled out because, since the HTMUs are not fatigue-resistant, it will be impossible to maintain a high rate of work for that duration and you will have to use a lighter load to complete the set. While the load used is not of prime importance with metabolic work, it still plays a role in stimulating positive adaptations. So it should be evident that the ideal set duration is between 20 and 60 seconds. Anecdotally I found that sets of 30-40 seconds produce the best results with metabolic work. So I do recommend this as a "baseline" time range. Shorter (20-30 seconds) and longer (40-60 seconds) sets can also be used from time to time, as a change of pace. Shorter sets being better suited for maximum growth phases and longer ones for fat loss phases.

What type of resistance should we use?

In my original "*Superman sets*" article I recommended using free-weights for timed sets. While these can still be used effectively, I find that an elastic source of resistance (e.g. elastic tubing with two handles) provides better results than free-weights. Why? Because it allows you to take advantage of the high-speed execution more so than the free-weights. With free-weights you must decelerate during a very important portion of the movement, this is done as a reflex to protect the joints from a ballistic shock; the faster you move, the more time you'll spend decelerating (and the less time you'll spend accelerating) because you'll need a longer breaking distance. This is not what we want! The elastic source of resistance acts as a break: the more you stretch it, the more resistance it provides. So the elastic tubing will do most of the deceleration job for you. As a result your nervous system will spend more time trying to accelerate. The elastic bands also allow you to return to the starting position faster, increasing the possible rate of work. Finally the tubing allows you to modify the resistance used during a set as fatigue sets in. When movement speed starts to slow down you can walk back so that the tubing will not be stretched as much, decreasing the amount of resistance and allowing you to maintain a high rate of work. As you can see, elastic tubing clearly is the superior choice of training equipment for metabolic work. However free-weights can still be used if no tubing is available to you.

How to use it?

While timed sets/metabolic work can be used as a stand-alone exercise, the greatest benefits are reached when it is supersetted with a regular lifting movement. For example after performing a set of incline dumbbell press you can move on to a low-position alternate punching metabolic movement. This type of training is incredibly effective at stimulating muscle growth, fat loss and power gains.

Key points

1. When performing timed sets/metabolic work you should emphasize speed of movement above all else.

2. When gaining size is your primary objective you should use sets of either 30-40 seconds or 20-30 seconds.

3. When losing fat is your primary objective you should use sets of either 30-40 seconds or 40-60 seconds.

4. An elastic resistance is superior to free-weights for high-speed metabolic work.

5. To get the most out of metabolic work, superset it with a regular lifting exercise. This is especially effective during a fat loss phase.

Effective metabolic exercises

It's pretty easy to come up with effective movements to use with this technique. The ones I will present are not your only options. As long as you use a high-speed of movement and the proper set duration, this technique will work. The following exercises are the ones that I use myself and with my clients. You will notice that in most cases I rely on unilateral exercises. This is both to increase HTMUs activation and to increase core involvement (unilateral work requires more stabilization) which also increases energy expenditure.

Metabolic exercise 1. Low-position alternate punching

Best used in conjunction with: Any type of incline pressing or incline flies

Metabolic exercise 2. High-position alternate punching

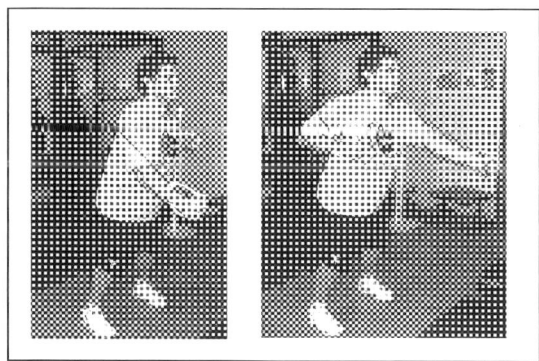

Best used in conjunction with: Any type of flat or decline pressing/flies

Metabolic exercise 3. Low-position alternate pulling

Best used in conjunction with: Any type of horizontal pulling exercise

Metabolic exercise 4. High-position alternate pulling

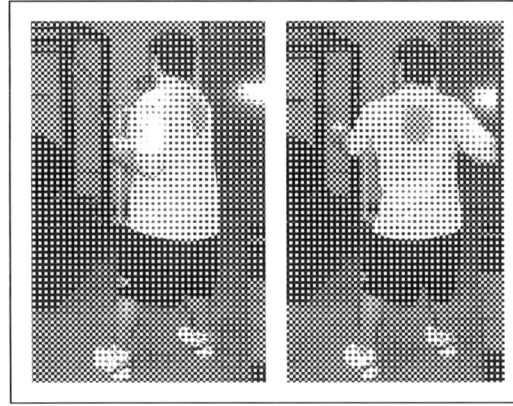

Best used in conjunction with: Any type of vertical pulling exercise

Metabolic exercise 5. Alternate shoulder punching

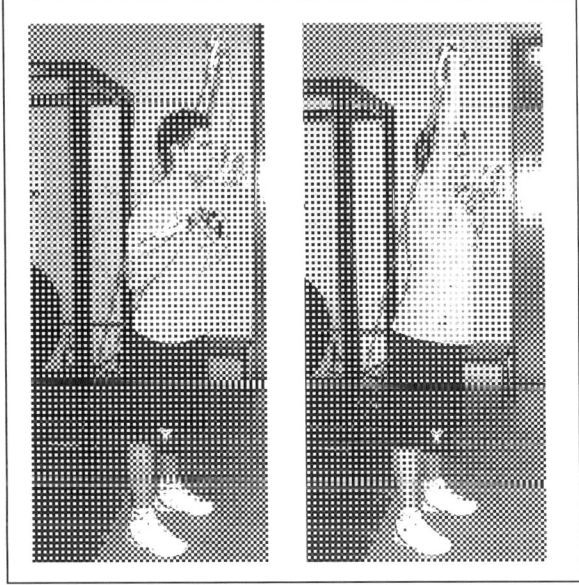

Best used in conjunction with: Any type of overhead pressing exercise

Metabolic exercise 6. Alternate front raise

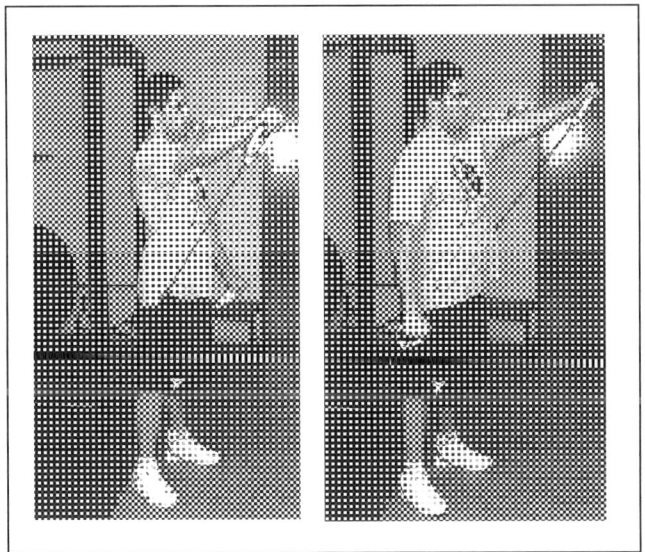

Best used in conjunction with: Any front raise exercise

Metabolic exercise 7. Lateral raise

Best used in conjunction with: Any lateral raise exercise

Metabolic exercise 8. Alternate upright rowing

Best used in conjunction with: Any variation of the upright row, Olympic lifts or shrug movements

Metabolic exercise 9. Alternate curl

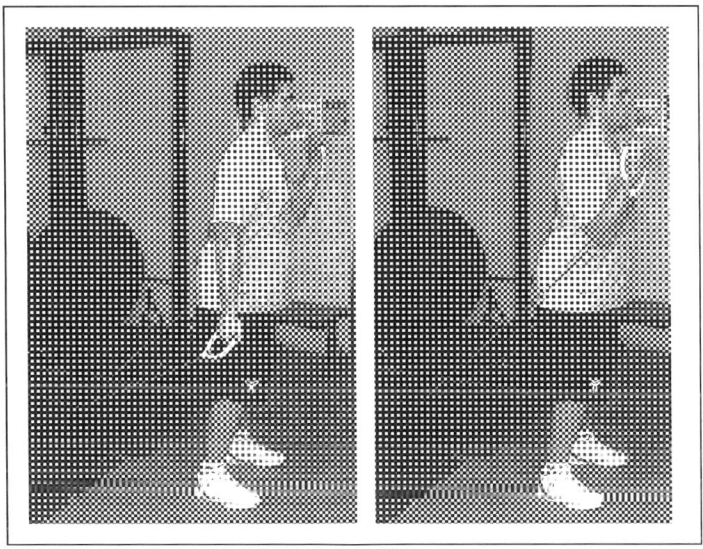

Best used in conjunction with: Any type of "palms up" curl

Metabolic exercise 10. Alternate reverse curl

Best used in conjunction with: Any type of "palms down" or hammer grip cur

Metabolic exercise 11. Alternate triceps extension

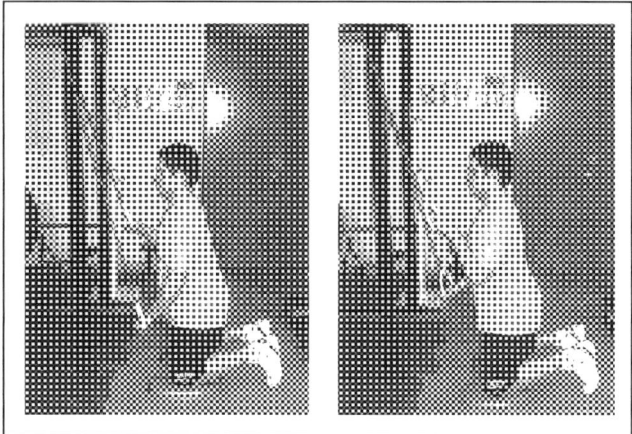

Best used in conjunction with: Any type of triceps work

Lower body metabolic work

For the lower body the tubing exercises aren't always ideal. Several different exercises can be used: sprints, series of jumps or high-speed lifting movements (squat for example) with a light load. Remember, speed and rate of work is what is most important.

PRINCIPLE 11
Eccentric loading and deceleration training for strength, power and size

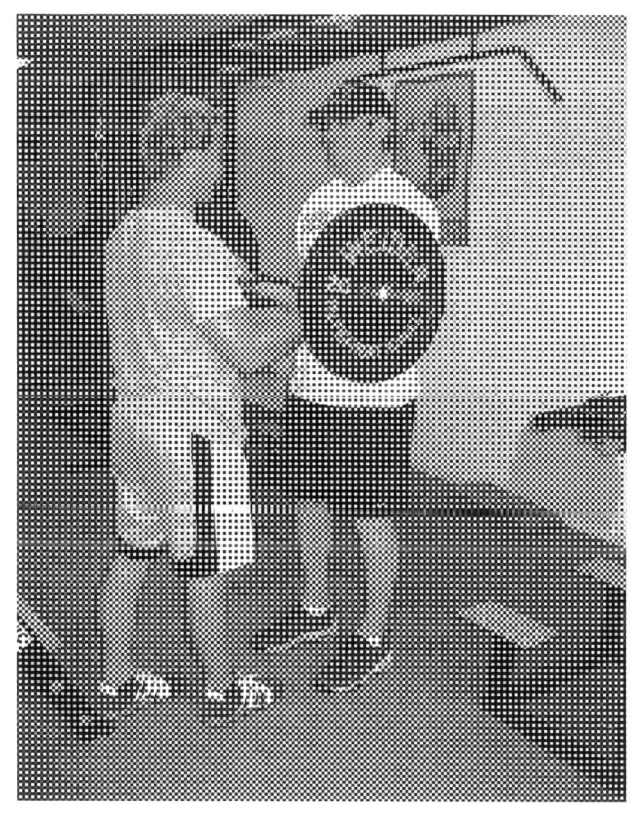

Introduction

We already saw that to maximize growth it is important to emphasize the eccentric portion of an exercise by performing the first ¾ of the lowering phase in a controlled and tensed fashion. In this chapter I will present several different accentuated eccentric methods that can be added to your program to elicit greater strength and size gains. However please understand that some of these methods are quite advanced and shouldn't be used by the beginner or by someone training alone without supervision.

Accentuated eccentric training is beneficial for athletes, bodybuilders as well as powerlifters/strength athletes. For athletes eccentric training is also "deceleration training"; it improves your body's capacity to absorb an external force and that is a key component of high level athletic performance (before being able to overcome a resistance you must first absorb and stop it). The bodybuilder will get the benefit of an increase in HTMUs stimulation since fast-twitch muscle fibers are recruited almost exclusively during this type of training; this will lead to a lot of direct muscle growth but also to an increase in growth potential by improving your neuromuscular capacity to recruit the "money" HTMUs. Finally, powerlifters will get a lot out of eccentric loading too by stimulating the strong and powerful fast-twitch fibers but also by getting their body used to handling heavy weights.

As you can see when properly applied eccentric training can be a worthy addition to almost any training program. There are several such methods you can use ranging from high-speed eccentric loading (a form of plyometric training) right up to supramaximal eccentrics. Each of these methods has their own potential benefits. By understanding these benefits you'll better be able to select the method that better suits your own needs. The following table adapted from *"Theory and Application of Modern Strength and Power Methods"* presents these different approaches to eccentric training.

There are several different eccentric training methods. But first understand that by eccentric training methods I mean those in which the eccentric portion of the exercise is emphasized, not necessarily exercises in which there is only an eccentric action taking place.

There are three main types of eccentric training, each with its own subtypes and applications. These three types of training are:

1. Submaximal eccentric training
2. Near-maximal and maximal eccentric training
3. Supramaximal eccentric training

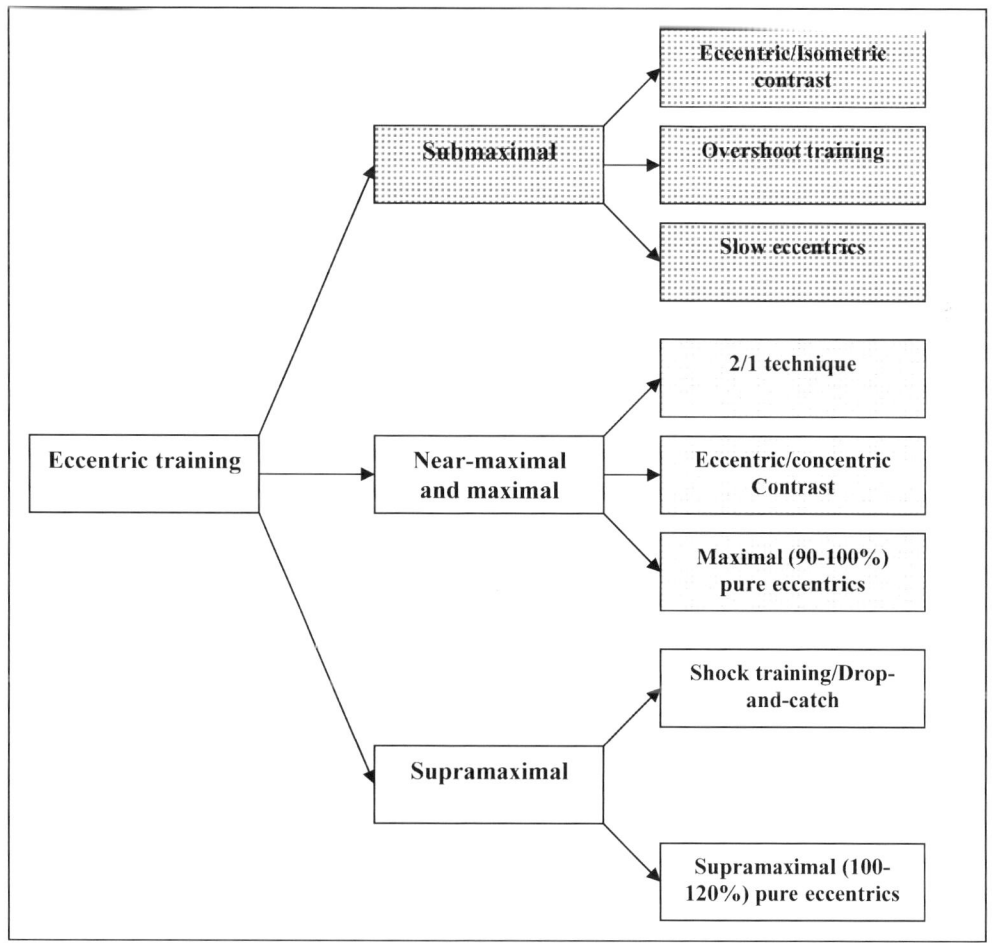

Submaximal eccentric training

With submaximal eccentric training you find yourself using a load that is lower than your maximum concentric strength. Since your maximum eccentric strength is significantly higher, the intensity of work will thus be submaximal. So to create a significant training effect we must use certain training techniques that will create an important stimulus, despite the relatively low intensity. I will present three of these techniques (although there are many more possibilities): **eccentric/isometric contrast**, **eccentric/concentric contrast**, and **slow eccentrics**.

Eccentric/isometric contrast (version A: stopped eccentrics)

In this type of exercise you find yourself slowly lowering a load equivalent to 60-80% of your maximum concentric strength in a movement, adding several isometric (static) pauses during the eccentric (lowering) portion; the longer the range of motion of an exercise, the more pauses you'll take. Each of these pauses should last 3 to 6 seconds. Once the bar has been fully lowered (eccentric portion of the movement is completed) you lift the bar or have a partner lift it for you. Normally sets of 1 to 5 reps are performed, obviously the more pauses you use (or the longer they are) and the heavier the weight is, the less reps you'll perform.

For big range of motion (ROM) compound movements (squats, deadlifts, etc.) you should use 3-4 pauses, for medium ROM compound movements (bench press, rowing, military press, etc.) you should use 2-3 pauses, and for short ROM exercises you should use 2 pauses. Note that this method will also be used in the "isometric methods" chapter since it does emphasize both types of muscle actions.

Eccentric/isometric contrast (version B: limit iso turn eccentric)

In this second version you will use a load equivalent to 70-90% of your concentric maximum on an exercise. You lower the bar slightly (usually to the strongest point in the range of motion) and you hold it there for as long as you can (maximum duration isometric effort). When you can no longer hold the weight statically you lower it as slowly as you can until you reach the end of the full range of motion. You then have a partner assist you in lifting the bar. Obviously only 1 rep is performed per set. This technique use a fatiguing isometric hold to "pre-fatigue" the muscles that will have to work harder during the subsequent eccentric action.

In both cases, exercises where the muscle is put in a full stretch position at the end of the eccentric phase are superior choices. These exercises were presented earlier in this book.

Overshoot training

Overshoot refers to an activation of fast-twitch motor units during the eccentric portion of the lift allowing the athlete to be more explosive during the concentric portion. In many regards this works the same way as depth jumps and other high impact plyometric drills. To perform an overshoot set you'll need either a set of weight releasers (see the upcoming eccentric/concentric contrast method for more on weight releasers) or have a partner apply pressure on the bar during the lowering phase of the first rep.

We accomplish this overshoot by lowering a heavy load during the eccentric portion and lifting a light load as fast as possible. We don't have to use a superslow eccentric phase, simply control the weight. Lowering the load in 2-3 seconds is adequate.

The bar weight should be around 50-60% of your concentric maximum and you should add another 30-40% on the releasers. For example, an athlete who can bench press 400lbs would use the following:

a. Bar weight = 400lbs x 50% = 200lbs
b. Releasers weight = 400lbs x 30% = 120lbs (60lbs per side)
Total weight = 320lbs/200lbs

We want to perform sets of 2-4 reps using this method. However, the releasers are only used on the first rep. The overshoot phenomenon is maintained for the whole set provided that acceleration is maintained at the maximum possible level. In other words, the first rep is performed with a heavier weight lowered under control followed by 2-4 explosive lifts.

Once again, if you do not have a set of weight releasers you can have your partner apply pressure on the bar as you lower it, and have him remove his hands as you lift the weight.

Superslow eccentrics

This technique is fairly simple. Using a moderate-to-important load (60-85% of your max) you execute a superslow yielding phase while lifting (overcoming) the bar explosively. You should lower the bar in 6-12 seconds depending on the weight. When training for size the number of reps per set will depend on your fiber makeup and lactate tolerance; aim for technical muscle failure on each set.

Near-maximal and maximal eccentric training

This method basically refers to lowering, *under control*, a load nearing (or at) the point of maximum strength.

I have included three basic techniques in the NM/M eccentric class of methods:

1. **The 2/1 technique**: Using a load that is 100-150% of the concentric strength of a single-limb exercise, do the eccentric/yielding portion with just that one limb (e.g. with only the right arm) and the concentric/overcoming portion with both limbs. For example if you can use 40lbs with one arm on the machine curl station, use 40-60lbs for your set: lift it explosively with two arms and lower it slowly with one arm. Perform 3-5 reps per arm (alternate on each rep).

2. **Ecentric/concentric contrast**: This form of training revolves around contrasting a relatively heavy or hard eccentric (lowering) phase with a much easier or more explosive concentric (lifting) one. The weight during the concentric phase should be around 70-80% of your maximum and extra loading is added during the eccentric phase either via a set of weight releasers or manual (partner) overload.

3. **Maximal pure eccentrics:** In this variation, commonly known as "negatives," you only perform the eccentric portion of an exercise and have a spotter lift the bar back to the starting position for you. Since this is not a supramaximal method you use 90-100% of your maximum and lower the bar under control in 5 seconds for sets of 2-5 reps.

In all three cases the purpose is always to lower a load close to your maximum capacity. The methods only vary in the way that you bring the weight back up to the starting position for another rep (or to conclude the set).

The 2/1 technique

This technique can be used quite effectively with exercises such as the seated row, cable rope curl, cable rope triceps extension, and most exercises that can be done using the triceps rope. It also works on most machines. The way it works is pretty simple: you lift the weight (overcoming/concentric portion) using two limbs (both arms if you are doing an upper body exercise, both legs if it's a lower body movement) and you return the weight (yielding/eccentric portion) with one limb.

So the load during the yielding portion of the exercise is twice as high as during the overcoming portion. The load to use should be light enough so that you can accelerate it during the overcoming portion but heavy enough to make the single-limb yielding portion hard to do. A load of around 70% of your "two-limb maximum" is a good place to start.

The overcoming portion should be done as fast as possible while the yielding portion is to be executed in 5 seconds. Sets of 3-5 reps per limb are performed (so 6-10 total reps per set).

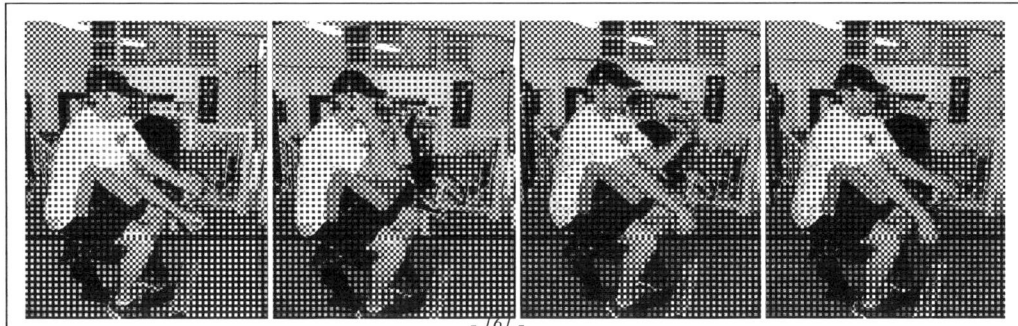

Eccentric/concentric contrast

This form of training revolves around contrasting a relatively heavy or hard eccentric (lowering) phase with a much easier or more explosive concentric (lifting) one. The best way to do this is to use weight releasers which are "hooks" suspended to the bar that unload as you reach the bottom portion of the eccentric phase.

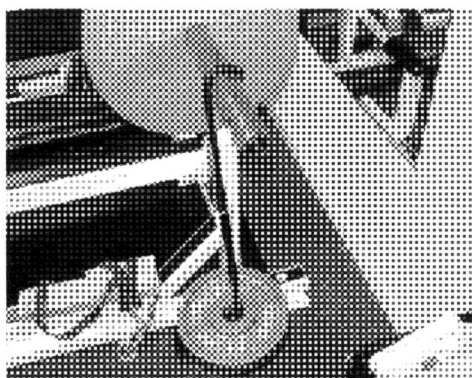 

Weight releasers are one of the most important tools that a coach can buy. Furthermore, they're inexpensive, which makes them a great deal! You can get them online at **www.elitefts.com**. I personally use this tool in the training of almost all of my athletes, and it constitutes a significant part of their yearly program.

Releasers are quite simple to understand. Basically we're talking about hooks which are attached to the bar and loaded with weight. The hooks hang down lower than the bar, so as you lower the bar, the releasers will make contact with the ground, allowing them to "unhook" from the bar, thus *releasing* the additional weight from the bar.

They thus allow an athlete to lower more weight than he lifts. As it was mentioned in the second principle section of this book, the eccentric portion of a movement is responsible for a lot of strength and size gains.

An alternative to the weight releasers is to have a partner push down on the bar during the eccentric portion of the lift. I've used this technique myself and it does work. However, it becomes very hard to quantify the training progress. How much resistance did you add during the eccentric portion? 35lbs, 45lbs, 100lbs? You can't really tell. So this method can be useful, but it has its limitations.

Releasers on the other hand allow you to add resistance during the eccentric portion of a lift and know exactly how much more you've added. This makes training quantification possible.

For example, below the first athlete has 455lbs on the bar, plus 65lbs of releasers per side (total of 130lbs). The second athlete has 315lbs on the bar plus 65lbs of releasers per side. Both perform 5 singles with that load. So they would write down the following in their journal:

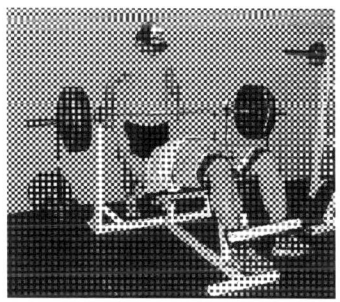 

5 x 1 @ 585/455   5 x 1 @ 445/315

As you can see, by using weight releasers you can know exactly what is going on with the athlete's training.

The first method of eccentric/concentric contrast is the **80% method**. With this method you simply use a bar weight that is 80% of the total load. For example if the combined weight the releasers and the bar is 400lbs then 80% of that is 320lbs. So that means that you should put 320lbs on the bar and 40lbs added as releaser weight on each side (each releasers weights 15lbs so you add an extra 25lbs on each one). You execute the eccentric portion under control, in 5 seconds or more. If you cannot lower the bar in 5 seconds, then the weight is too heavy. If it's easy to lower it in 5 seconds you can add some weight.

So to recap, our athlete with a max of 400lbs choosing to train at 80% would use a bar weight of 320lbs and add 25lbs to each releaser. This way he lowers 100% and lifts 80% of his maximum.

This training method should be performed for multi-rep sets. Since the releasers must be replaced on each repetition I suggest two approaches:

1. **Cluster training**: perform 5-8 single reps with around 5-10 seconds of rest between them. After each rep you rack the bar and replace the releasers (or have a partner replace them).

2. **Paused training**: perform 5-8 reps, but after each rep hold the bar at arms length while two partners simultaneously replace the releasers.

I prefer option 1 myself. Option 2 is a bit riskier, because if the releasers are replaced with even a slight delay between them an injury may result. However, option 2 has the advantage of keeping the muscles under load for a longer period of time, which may be slightly better for hypertrophy purposes.

As I previously mentioned you can use a manual overload instead of the releasers: your partner will have to push down on the bar during the eccentric portion of the movement then release it as you execute the lifting portion. While this method has the shortcoming of being less precise than the weight releasers (because you don't know exactly how much pressure the partner is applying) it does have and upside too; since you don't have the pause between reps, the manual overload method is probably better for stimulating muscle growth. It also allows you to perform more reps per set as your partner can decrease the amount of pressure he puts on the bar to accommodate your fatigue accumulation as the set progresses.

Maximal pure eccentrics

This method uses loads that are between 90 and 100% of your maximum on a given lift that you only perform the eccentric portion of the exercise; your partner generously helping you to bring the bar back to the starting position. The eccentric portion should be performed in 5 seconds or more, you continue to perform reps until it is no longer possible to control the weight for that long. Normally that will be 3-4 reps with 90-95% and 1-2 reps with 95-100%.

Supramaximal eccentric training

During a supramaximal eccentric set, the muscles and tendons are placed under a stress that is higher than what is normally seen in a maximal voluntary concentric movement. This is done either by absorbing and abruptly stopping a falling load (shock training and drop & catch method), by performing a high speed eccentric action (overspeed eccentrics) or my lowering a load that is heavier than your concentric maximum (supra max eccentrics with 100-120%). In all three of these methods the muscles have to produce a level of tension that exceeds what is normally seen in a maximal lift. This obviously has a tremendous training effect on the nervous system and muscular structure.

Shock training and drop & catch method

As we saw earlier, shock training refers to plyometric work. I will not repeat myself as I don't want to sound like a senile grandfather! Suffice to say that the way shock training works is my creating both a very important loaded pre-stretch and muscle activation/stiffness which will increase the power production of a subsequent explosive movement. Shock training (and the drop & catch method that we will see in a few minutes) constitute a form of supramaximal eccentric work because of the large force sustained by the muscles upon reception. For example, during a depth jump the external resistance from the accumulated kinetic energy can be as high as 6 times your bodyweight upon landing.

The <u>drop & catch</u> as well as the <u>drop, catch & lift</u> methods are basically plyometric work with weights. I personally refer to this type of training as deceleration/breaking training (drop & catch) or breaking-overcoming (drop, catch & lift) training. The basic premise is the same as during plyometric work: you increase the external resistance by having a body accumulate kinetic energy as it falls down (in the case of plyos the source of resistance is your own body while with the drop & catch method it's a barbell) then absorb its force by abruptly stopping its downward progression (you do so by making your muscles super stiff immediately upon reception) then follow it by an explosive concentric/lifting action (if it's a drop, catch & lift exercise). Below is an illustration of a few drop and catch exercises. Understand that the falling down phase is super short because you really must "attack" the weight as it falls down and abruptly stop its downward progression so the picture quality might not be worthy of Annie Lebowitz! However I think that you'll still get the big picture.

Drop & catch curl

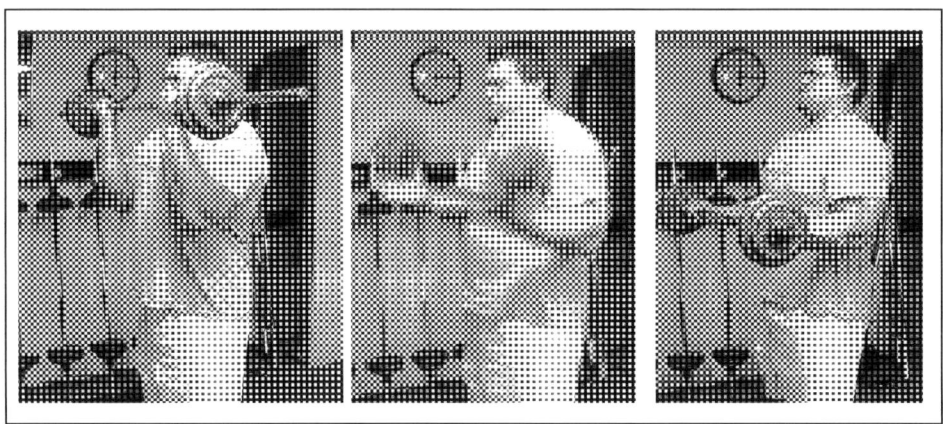

Key point(s): Catch the bar with the arms bent at a 90 degrees angle. <u>Immediately</u> as the bar touches your hands (during the reception) you must tense your muscles as hard as possible so that you stop the falling barbell as fast as possible. In the drop & catch version you keep the biceps tensed hard with the elbows at 90 degrees for 3-5 seconds before returning to the starting position.

Drop, catch & lift curl

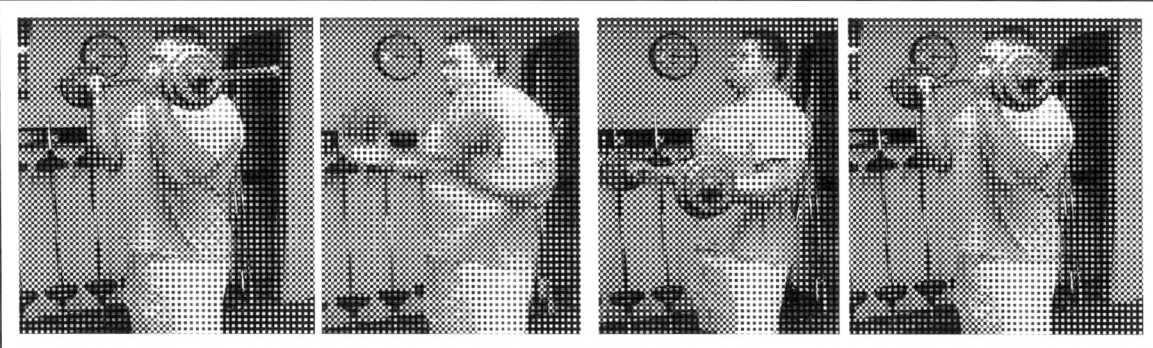

Key point(s): Catch the bar with the arms bent at a 90 degrees angle. Immediately as the bar touches your hands (during the reception) you must tense your muscles as hard as possible so that you stop the falling barbell as fast as possible. In the drop, catch & lift variation you explode back up to the starting position as soon as you catch the bar. Still take your time between reps to make sure that the movement is of a high quality.

Drop & catch barbell rowing

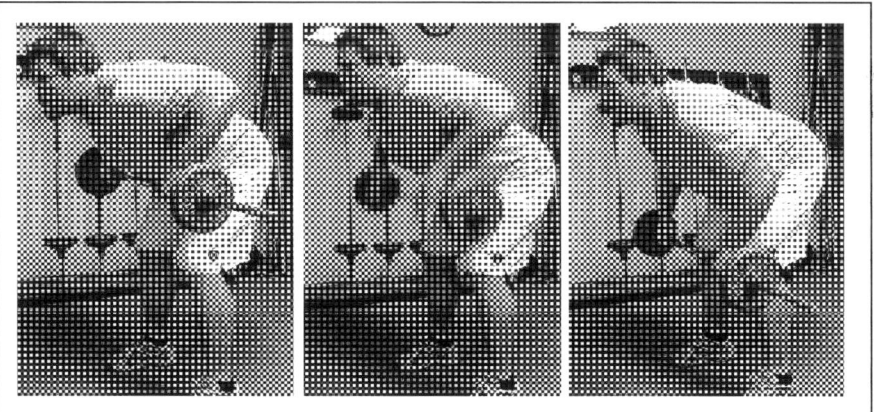

Key point(s): Catch the bar with the elbows bent at 90 degrees. Immediately upon reception of the bar you must tense not only your arms but your back as hard as you can. In the drop & catch version, as you catch the bar, hold the reception position for 3-5 seconds, keeping your back as tightly tensed as possible before returning to the starting position.

Drop, catch & lift barbell rowing

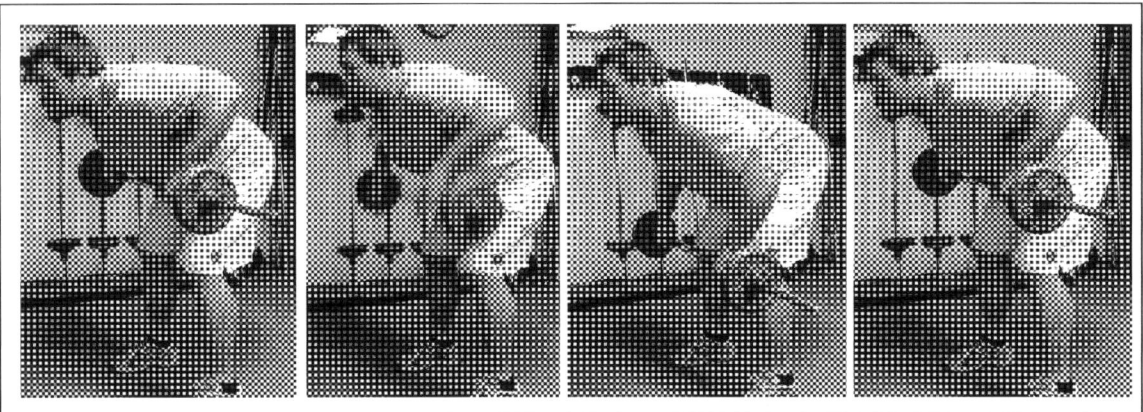

Key point(s): Catch the bar with the elbows bent at 90 degrees. Immediately upon reception of the bar you must tense not only your arms but your back as hard as you can. In the drop, catch and lift variation you explode back up to the starting position as soon as you catch the bar. Still take your time between reps to make sure that the movement is of a high quality.

Drop & catch front raise

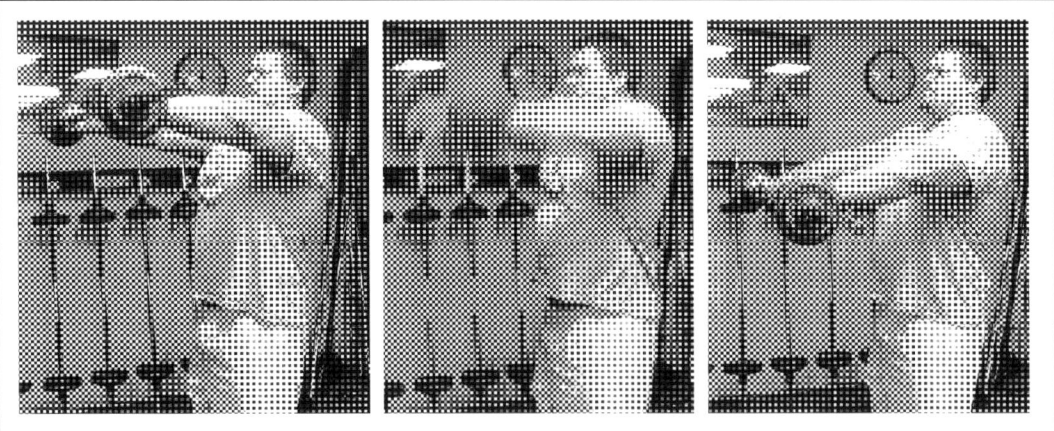

Key point(s): Drop the bar and catch it at arms length when it's down to the upper portion of the abdomen. As with the previous exercises, stop the downward progression as abruptly as possible by forcefully tensing the deltoids immediately as you catch the bar. In the drop & catch variation you hold the low position for 3-5 seconds while contracting your deltoids as hard as you can before returning to the starting position.

Drop, catch & lift front raise

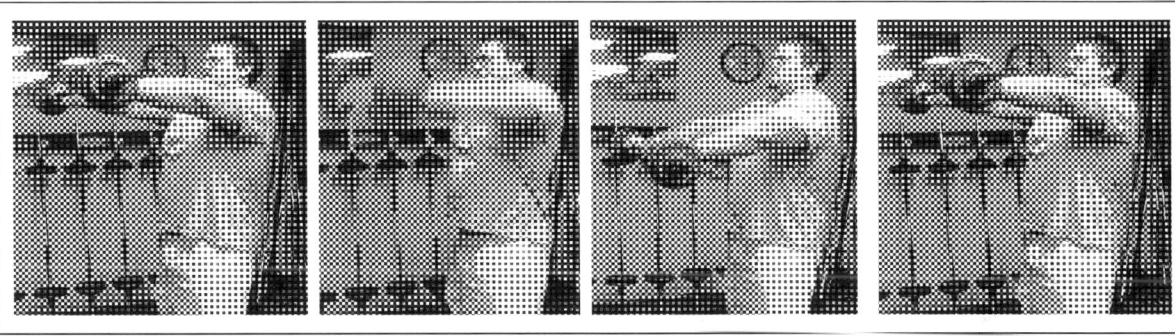

Key point(s): Drop the bar and catch it at arms length when it's down to the upper portion of the abdomen. As with the previous exercises, stop the downward progression as abruptly as possible by forcefully tensing the deltoids immediately as you catch the bar. In the drop, catch & lift variation you explode back up to the starting position as soon as you catch the bar. Still take your time between reps to make sure that the movement is of a high quality.

These are just a few examples, most lifts performed with a barbell can be performed as a drop & catch movement (although I would personally recommend NOT doing drop & catch overhead presses!) as long as the stiff absorption rule is respected.

Other movements include: drop & catch bench press, drop & catch incline press, drop & catch decline press, drop and catch upright row, drop & catch squat, drop & catch lunges, etc.

Remember that the load you use isn't as important as the stiffness you are able to produce upon reception. If you have to absorb the bar by following its downward movement as you catch it (not stopping it abruptly) then the load is excessive for your current level of deceleration strength.

Supra-maximal pure eccentrics

This method uses loads that are between 100 and 120% of your concentric maximum on a given lift and you only perform the eccentric portion of the exercise; your partner generously helping you to bring the bar back to the starting position. The eccentric portion should be performed in 5 seconds or more. If you cannot lower the weight under control in 5 seconds, then the load is too heavy. Only single repetitions should be used when the supra-maximal pure eccentrics method is employed. Anyway you should very rarely rely on this type of training. Only highly trained athletes should use it, and not very often. Obviously weight releasers can also be used for this method, all that was said about this approach still applies; only the amount of weight on the releasers (heavier) and the number of reps per ser (only 1) with change.

Exercises organisation

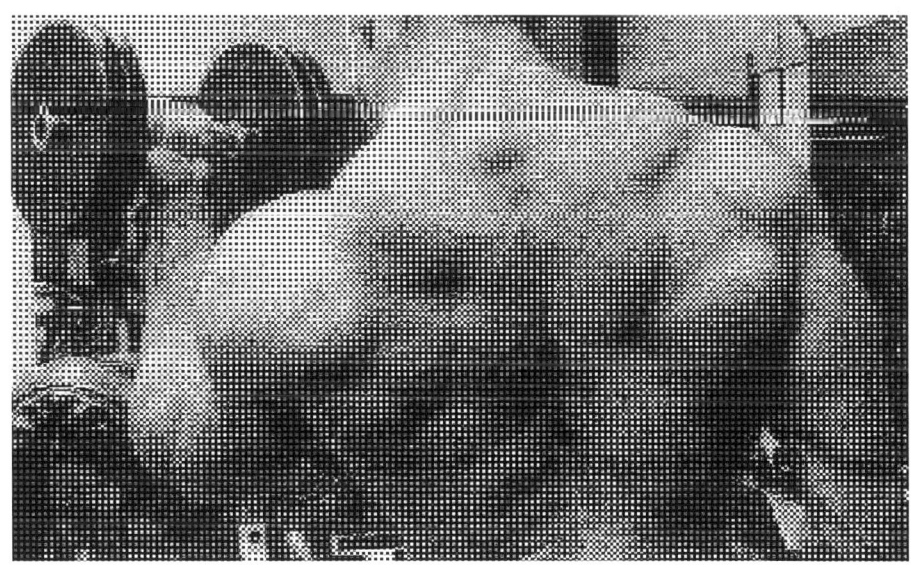

Introduction

In the preceding chapters we saw the most effective exercises to stimulate muscle growth in each of the major muscle groups. I have also detailed several types of exercises:

Activation: Exercises that serve the purpose of increasing neural activation of a certain muscle group. Indirectly these movements are also useful for athletes via their positive effect on balance and stability. These drills are most often performed on unstable surfaces.

Potentiation: Exercises that focus on neural facilitation, also called post-tetanic potentiation and high frequency initial pulse potentiation. Simply put, these explosive exercises lead to a greater muscle recruitment and force production during subsequent exercises. Note that plyometric work as well as the drop & catch and drop, catch & lift methods are to be included in our list of potentiation exercises.

Stimulation: Exercises aimed at stimulating muscle growth. These movements are the ones better suited to maximally recruit the HTMUs of the targeted muscle group which will lead to the greatest muscle growth possible.

Metabolic: Exercises performed at a high rate of work for a prescribed period of time (20-60 seconds). The objective is to perform as much physical work as possible within that given time frame. This type of training increases energy expenditure and improves the efficiency of the glycolitic energy system.

To that we can add the various accentuated eccentric exercises.

There are several ways to organize these different types of exercises; they can either be performed as a stand-alone, a superset or a giant set depending on your objective. In this chapter I will describe the possible combinations that you can use when you design a training program.

Stand-alone activation exercise

When you perform an activation exercise by itself you do it either to "wake-up" the nervous system at the beginning of a workout or to work on stability and balance. If your main objective is to build muscle mass the first aspect is probably the most important to you. For that reason if you decide to use a stand-alone activation exercise, do it first in your workout so that it can be used to improve the efficacy of the rest of the training program.

Stand-alone potentiation exercise

Much like an activation movement, a potentiation one can "wake-up" the neuromuscular system when performed first in a workout. These explosive exercises can thus improve workout performance when done early in a workout. In most cases they also have a certain training effect of their own, mainly on power gains. If you use both a stand-alone potentiation and activation exercise in your workout you should start with the activation movement then move on to the potentiation drill. If you only perform the potentiation stand-alone, then do it first in your workout.

Stand-alone stimulation exercise

These represent the bulk of most muscle-building programs. Their main objective is to stimulate muscle growth; to do so optimally you should perform sets either in the functional hypertrophy (6-8), total hypertrophy (8-12) or strength-endurance (12-15) rep ranges.

Stand-alone metabolic exercise

The metabolic work/timed sets are really designed to be performed as part of a superset with a stimulation or potentiation exercise. By itself it can be a decent anaerobic conditioning tool for athletes involved in sports where short but intense actions are needed. But when it comes to body composition changes, it really needs to be used as part of a superset.

Activation + Stimulation superset (Pre-activation superset)

This mode of organisation uses two exercises for a muscle group performed as a superset (no rest between exercise A and exercise B). In a pre-activation superset we use the activation movement first then perform the stimulation exercise. For example we could perform 10 push-ups with the hands on a swiss ball then 8 to 10 reps in the bench press. This approach is best used when someone has problems recruiting a targeted muscle group during a stimulation exercise. For example if you have trouble getting a proper pectoral stimulation from a bench press, performing the swiss ball push-ups first will improve pectoral recruitment and thus make them more involved in the bench press. On the downside the activation exercise will also fatigue the muscles involved and thus might lead to a lesser growth stimulation. So this approach is best used only to solve "muscle recruitment" problems.

Stimulation + activation superset (Post-activation superset)

This is similar to the preceding technique in that you are supersetting a stimulation and an activation movement. However this time you perform the stimulation exercise first. The activation exercise will allow you to "finish off" an understimulated muscle by recruiting those last resilient muscle fibers that haven't been thoroughly fatigued by the stimulation movement. This approach will also allow you to use more weight on the stimulation exercise which will lead to a greater growth stimulus. Obviously for the first set we won't get a potentiating effect since there is no activation drill preceding the first set of the stimulation exercise. However the other sets (2nd, 3rd, 4th, etc.) will be potentiated by the activation exercise of the preceding set since the effect can last for up to 3 minutes after the completion of the movement.

Potentiation + Stimulation superset (Pre-potentiation superset)

This type of superset is pretty common in the world of athletic training; a power exercise being supersetted with a heavy exercise. This is known as "complex training". For muscle-building purposes this type of superset acts pretty much like an "activation + stimulation" superset with the same pros and cons. And added benefit is that most potentiation exercises do have a significant training effect on power production capacity, hypertrophy or both. Just like with the "activation + stimulation" superset the problem lies in the fact that the potentiation exercise can create some fatigue that might interfere with the performance of the stimulation exercise. When using light potentiation exercises like plyometric work, projection push-ups or medicine ball throws it isn't a problem to start with the potentiation movement though as these drills won't cause too much muscle fatigue.

Stimulation + Potentiation superset (Post-potentiation superset)

The same things that applies for the "stimulation + activation superset" applies here too. The benefits are pretty much the same as with the "potentiation + stimulation superset" without the effect of fatigue on the performance of the stimulation exercise. The potentiation movement will still have some benefits since the facilitating effect can last for 3-5 minutes.

Potentiation + Metabolic superset (power-endurance superset)

This exercise coupling is better suited for athletic development than for stimulating muscle growth. It is especially effective for athletes involved in sports requiring power-endurance (high level of power production sustained for a period of 30-60 seconds) such as ice hockey, 200-400m sprinting, gymnastics, figure skating, etc. The potentiation exercise allows you to develop peak power output while the high-speed metabolic work focuses more on the anaerobic capacity/power-endurance.

Stimulation + Metabolic superset (strength-endurance superset)

This method is very effective to stimulate positive body composition chanes. It will have a very powerful effect on growth stimulation but thoroughly stimulating the HTMUs and the metabolic component also favors fat mobilization and fat loss.

Activation + Stimulation + Metabolic giant set (organic giant set 1)

All four organic giant sets can be used either for fat-loss or muscle growth purposes in an intermediate or advanced level program. This first organic giant set is particularly effective in the case of a underdeveloped muscle group rendered stubborn because its synergists are dominating (e.g. weak chest because of strong shoulders).

Potentiation + Stimulation + Metabolic giant set (organic giant set 2)
This type of giant set will indeed lead to muscle size gains and some fat loss. But its fundamental purpose is probably in the training of athletes as it allows for the development of power, strength and anaerobic capacity all at once in a pattern that is similar to that found in sports (e.g. think of an offensive lineman the powerful start at the snap is followed by a strength effort when battling with his opponent and as the play continue he will require more and more anaerobic capacity to sustain his level of performance).

Stimulation + Activation + Metabolic giant set (organic giant set 3)
Of all the organic giant sets, this is the one that will lead to the better overall change in body composition.. Putting the stimulation exercise first, when you are relatively fresh, will allow you to use more weight and get a stronger muscle contraction. The activation exercise will then prime you for the metabolic exercise while tapping into the last remaining HTMUs.

Stimulation + Stimulation + Metabolic giant set (organic giant set 4)
This is the best approach to stimulate a maximum amount of muscle growth. You utilize two stimulation exercises (one compound/multi-joint and one isolation) and a metabolic exercise for the same muscle group.

Potentiation + Stimulation + Activation + Metabolic giant set (thorough giant set)
This giant set is better kept for fat loss phases in advanced individuals as it requires a very high work capacity. It's not something that you can jump into without gradually building your capacity to handle physical stress. To do well on this type of giant set you must have a pretty good level of general conditioning. While some muscle growth may occur when using this approach, it should not be expected as this method is more effective at stimulating fat loss and improving anaerobic conditioning. It can also be a

very good addition in the training program of athletes who must perform a lot of intensive work for 2-3 minutes (boxers, mixed martial artists, wrestlers, etc.).

Key points regarding program design

1. Regardless of the exercise being performed, the load used or the fatigue level, you should always attempt to generate as much force as possible during each concentric repetition.

2. Except for potentiation exercises, every eccentric repetition should be performed not only under control, but while actively flexing the muscles.

3. You must precede every concentric repetition by a stretch of the targeted muscle group. A set should be like this: controlled and flexed (first 3/4 eccentric); stretch (last ¼ eccentric); explode! (concentric)

4. Choose the best exercises to do the job. Exercise selection is very important and should not be taken lightly.

5. If you want to wake-up the nervous system you can add an activation or potentiation exercise to your program.

6. If you want to increase fat loss while building muscle you can add some high-speed metabolic work to your program

Examples of training templates

The following templates will show you how to design your own workouts using the methods presented so far in this book. Obviously, depending on your goal, the training structure and organization will vary.

Muscle gain templates

For muscle growth purposes you should start training each muscle group at a twice-per-week frequency (shoulders and arms can be trained only once since they receive a lot of indirect stimulation from the other training days). Depending on your recovery capacity, work schedule and nutritional intake you'll have to split this weekly volume into 3 to 6 sessions. This is the template <u>for each muscle group</u>. If you train two muscle groups per session you use the template for both muscles; if you train three muscle groups you use the template for all three of these trained muscle groups, etc. Obviously these are just sample templates, feel free to utilize the information provided as you see fit.

Muscle growth template – Beginner level		
Exercise	Method	Loading scheme
1.	Activation exercise	3-4 sets of 8-10 reps (or max reps if it's an unloaded movement)
2.	Stimulation exercise (multi-joint or stronger exercise)	3-4 sets of 10 to 12 reps
3a.	Stimulation + Activation superset	3-4 sets of 10 to 12 reps
3b.		3-4 sets of maximum reps
4.	Stimulation exercise (isolation)	3-4 sets of 12 to 15 reps

Muscle growth template – Intermediate level		
Exercise	Method	Loading scheme
1a.	Activation + Stimulation superset	3-4 sets of maximum reps
1b.		3-4 sets of 10 to 12 reps
2.	Stimulation exercise (multi-joint or stronger exercise)	3-4 sets of 8 to 10 reps
3a.	Stimulation (MJ) + Stimulation (ISO) superset	3-4 sets of 8 to 10 reps
3b.		3-4 sets of 10 to 12 reps

Muscle growth template – Advanced level		
Exercise	Method	Loading scheme
1a.	Activation + Stimulation superset	3-4 sets of maximum reps
1b.		3-4 sets of 8 to 10 reps
2a.	Potentiation + stimulation superset	3-4 sets of 8 to 10 reps
2b.		3-4 sets of 6 to 8 reps
3a.	Stimulation (MJ) + Stimulation (ISO) + Metabolic giant set	3-4 sets of 8 to 10 reps
3b.		3-4 sets of 10 to 12 reps
3c.		3-4 sets of 20-30 seconds

Fat loss template – Beginner level		
Exercise	Method	Loading scheme
1a.	Activation + Metabolic superset	3-4 sets of maximum reps
1b.		3-4 sets of 30 to 40 seconds
2a.	Stimulation + Metabolic superset	3-4 sets of 12 to 15 reps
2b.		3-4 sets of 30-40 seconds.
3a.	Stimulation + Metabolic superset	3-4 sets of 12 to 15 reps
3b.		3-4 sets of 30-40 seconds.

Fat loss template – Intermediate level		
Exercise	Method	Loading scheme
1a.	Activation + Metabolic superset	3-4 sets of maximum reps
1b.		3-4 sets of 30 to 40 seconds
2a.	Stimulation + Metabolic superset	3-4 sets of 12 to 15 reps
2b.		3-4 sets of 30-40 seconds.
3a.	Stimulation + Activation + Metabolic giant set	3-4 sets of 12 to 15 reps
3b.		3-4 sets of maximum reps
3c.		3-4 sets of 30-40 seconds

Fat loss template – Advanced level		
Exercise	Method	Loading scheme
1a.	Activation + Metabolic superset	3-4 sets of maximum reps
1b.		3-4 sets of 30 to 40 seconds
2a.	Stimulation + Activation + Metabolic giant set	3-4 sets of 12 to 15 reps
2b.		3-4 sets of maximum reps
2c.		3-4 sets of 30-40 seconds
3a.	Stimulation (MJ) + Stimulation (ISO) + Metabolic giant set	3-4 sets of 12 to 15 reps
3b.		3-4 sets of 15 to 20 reps
3c.		3-4 sets of 30-40 seconds

General strength template – Beginner level		
Exercise	Method	Loading scheme
1.	Activation exercise	3-4 sets of maximum reps
2.	Potentiation exercise	3-4 sets of 6 to 8 reps
3.	Stimulation (main) exercise	4-5 sets of 4-6 reps
4.	Stimulation (assistance) exercise	3-4 sets of 6 to 8 reps

General strength template – Intermediate level		
Exercise	Method	Loading scheme
1.	Activation exercise	3-4 sets of maximum reps
2.	Potentiation exercise	3-4 sets of 6 to 8 reps
3.	Stimulation (main) exercise	5-6 sets of 2-4 reps
4.	Stimulation (assistance) exercise	4-5 sets of 4 to 6 reps

	General strength template – Advanced level	
Exercise	Method	Loading scheme
1.	Potentiation exercise	3-4 sets of 6 to 8 reps
2.	Stimulation (main) exercise	5-6 sets of 1-3 reps
3.	Potentiation exercise	3-4 sets of 6 to 8 reps
4.	Stimulation (assistance) exercise	4-5 sets of 3 to 5 reps

* Note that for the following powerlifting workouts I recommend using an Ed Coan split of squat, bench, deadlift, bench (4 weekly workouts).

	Powerlifting template – Beginner level (bench press workout)	
Exercise	Method	Loading scheme
1.	Activation exercise	3-4 sets of maximum reps
2.	Stimulation (bench variation) exercise	4-5 sets of 4-6 reps
3.	Stimulation (chest) exercise	3-4 sets of 6 to 8 reps
4.	Stimulation (triceps) exercise	3-4 sets of 6 to 8 reps
5.	Stimulation (delts) exercise	3-4 sets of 6 to 8 reps

	Powerlifting template – Beginner level (deadlift workout)	
Exercise	Method	Loading scheme
1.	Activation exercise	3-4 sets of maximum reps
2.	Stimulation (deadlift variation) exercise	4-5 sets of 4-6 reps
3.	Stimulation (hams) exercise	3-4 sets of 6 to 8 reps
4.	Stimulation (back) exercise	3-4 sets of 6 to 8 reps
5.	Stimulation (low back) exercise	3-4 sets of 10 to 12 reps
6.	Stimulation (biceps) exercise	3-4 sets of 10 to 12 reps

	Powerlifting template – Beginner level (squat workout)	
Exercise	Method	Loading scheme
1.	Activation exercise	3-4 sets of maximum reps
2.	Stimulation (squat variation) exercise	4-5 sets of 4-6 reps
3.	Stimulation (quads) exercise	3-4 sets of 6 to 8 reps
4.	Stimulation (back) exercise	3-4 sets of 6 to 8 reps
5.	Stimulation (low back) exercise	3-4 sets of 6 to 8 reps

Powerlifting template – Intermediate level (bench press workout)

Exercise	Method	Loading scheme
1.	Activation exercise	3-4 sets of maximum reps
2.	Potentiation exercise	3-4 sets of 6 to 8 reps
3.	Stimulation (bench variation) exercise	5-6 sets of 2-4 reps
4.	Stimulation (chest) exercise	3-4 sets of 4 to 6 reps
5.	Stimulation (triceps) exercise	3-4 sets of 4 to 6 reps
6.	Stimulation (delts) exercise	3-4 sets of 6 to 8 reps

Powerlifting template – Intermediate level (deadlift workout)

Exercise	Method	Loading scheme
1.	Activation exercise	3-4 sets of maximum reps
2.	Potentiation exercise	3-4 sets of 6 to 8 reps
3.	Stimulation (deadlift variation) exercise	5-6 sets of 2-4 reps
4.	Stimulation (hams) exercise	3-4 sets of 4 to 6 reps
5.	Stimulation (back) exercise	3-4 sets of 4 to 6 reps
6.	Stimulation (low back) exercise	3-4 sets of 8 to 10 reps
7.	Stimulation (biceps) exercise	3-4 sets of 8 to 10 reps

Powerlifting template – Intermediate level (squat workout)

Exercise	Method	Loading scheme
1.	Activation exercise	3-4 sets of maximum reps
2.	Potentiation exercise	3-4 sets of 6 to 8 reps
3.	Stimulation (squat variation) exercise	5-6 sets of 2-4 reps
4.	Stimulation (quads) exercise	3-4 sets of 4 to 6 reps
5.	Stimulation (back) exercise	3-4 sets of 4 to 6 reps
6.	Stimulation (low back) exercise	3-4 sets of 8 to 10 reps

Powerlifting template – Advanced level (bench press workout)

Exercise	Method	Loading scheme
1.	Potentiation exercise	3-4 sets of 6 to 8 reps
2.	Stimulation (bench variation) exercise	5-6 sets of 1-3 reps
3.	Eccentric exercise	Depends on the method
4.	Stimulation (chest) exercise	3-4 sets of 3 to 5 reps
5.	Stimulation (triceps) exercise	3-4 sets of 3 to 5 reps
6.	Stimulation (delts) exercise	3-4 sets of 6 to 8 reps

Powerlifting template – Advanced level (deadlift workout)		
Exercise	Method	Loading scheme
1.	Potentiation exercise	3-4 sets of 6 to 8 reps
2.	Stimulation (deadlift variation) exercise	5-6 sets of 1-3 reps
3.	Eccentric exercise	Depends on the method
4.	Stimulation (hams) exercise	3-4 sets of 3 to 5 reps
5.	Stimulation (back) exercise	3-4 sets of 3 to 5 reps
6.	Stimulation (low back) exercise	3-4 sets of 6 to 8 reps
7.	Stimulation (biceps) exercise	3-4 sets of 6 to 8 reps

Powerlifting template – Advanced level (squat workout)		
Exercise	Method	Loading scheme
1.	Potentiation exercise	3-4 sets of 6 to 8 reps
2.	Stimulation (squat variation) exercise	5-6 sets of 1-3 reps
3.	Eccentric exercise	Depends on the method
4.	Stimulation (quads) exercise	3-4 sets of 3 to 5 reps
5.	Stimulation (back) exercise	3-4 sets of 3 to 5 reps
6.	Stimulation (low back) exercise	3-4 sets of 6 to 8 reps

* Note that for the following athletic programs I suggest using an upper/lower training split.

Athletic template – Beginner level (lower body workout)		
Exercise	Method	Loading scheme
1a.	Activation (quads) +	3-4 sets of maximum reps
1b.	Activation (hams) superset	3-4 sets of maximum reps
2.	Potentiation (quads) exercise	3-4 sets of 6-8 reps
3.	Stimulation (quads) exercise	3-4 sets of 8 to 10 reps
4.	Potentiation (hams) exercise	3-4 sets of 6-8 reps
5.	Stimulation (hams) exercise	3-4 sets of 8 to 10 reps

Athletic template – Beginner level (upper body workout)

Exercise	Method	Loading scheme
1a.	Activation (push) +	3-4 sets of maximum reps
1b.	Activation (pull) superset	3-4 sets of maximum reps
2.	Potentiation (horizontal push) exercise	3-4 sets of 6-8 reps
3.	Stimulation (horizontal push) exercise	3-4 sets of 8 to 10 reps
4.	Stimulation (horizontal pull) exercise	3-4 sets of 6-8 reps
5.	Stimulation (vertical pull) exercise	3-4 sets of 8 to 10 reps
6.	Potentiation (vertical push) exercise	3-4 sets of 6-8 reps
7.	Stimulation (vertical push) exercise	3-4 sets of 8 to 10 reps

Athletic template – Intermediate level (lower body workout)

Exercise	Method	Loading scheme
1a.	Activation (quads) +	3-4 sets of maximum reps
1b.	Activation (hams) superset	3-4 sets of maximum reps
2a.	Potentiation +	3-4 sets of 6-8 reps
2b.	Stimulation (quads) superset	3-4 sets of 6 to 8 reps
3a.	Potentiation +	3-4 sets of 6-8 reps
3b.	Stimulation (hams) superset	3-4 sets of 6 to 8 reps

Athletic template – Intermediate level (upper body workout)

Exercise	Method	Loading scheme
1a.	Activation (push) +	3-4 sets of maximum reps
1b.	Activation (pull) superset	3-4 sets of maximum reps
2a.	Potentiation +	3-4 sets of 6-8 reps
2b.	Stimulation (horizontal push) superset	3-4 sets of 6 to 8 reps
3.	Stimulation (horizontal pull) exercise	3-4 sets of 6-8 reps
4.	Stimulation (vertical pull) exercise	3-4 sets of 6 to 8 reps
5a.	Potentiation +	3-4 sets of 6-8 reps
5b.	Stimulation (vertical push) superset	3-4 sets of 6 to 8 reps

Athletic template – Advanced level (lower body workout)		
Exercise	Method	Loading scheme
1a.	Activation (quads) +	3-4 sets of maximum reps
1b.	Activation (hams) superset	3-4 sets of maximum reps
2a.	Potentiation +	4-5 sets of 6-8 reps
2b.	Stimulation + Metabolic	4-5 sets of 6 to 8 reps (or 4 to 6)
2c.	(quads) giant set	4-5 sets of 20-30 seconds
3a.	Potentiation +	4-5 sets of 6-8 reps
3b.	Stimulation + Metabolic	4-5 sets of 6 to 8 reps (or 4 to 6)
3c.	(hams) giant set	4-5 sets of 20-30 seconds

Athletic template – Advanced level (upper body workout)		
Exercise	Method	Loading scheme
1a.	Activation (push) +	3-4 sets of maximum reps
1b.	Activation (pull) superset	3-4 sets of maximum reps
2a.	Potentiation +	3-4 sets of 6-8 reps
2b.	Stimulation + Metabolic	3-4 sets of 6 to 8 reps (or 4 to 6)
2c.	(horizontal push) giant set	3-4 sets of 20-30 seconds
3.	Stimulation (horizontal pull) exercise	4-5 sets of 6-8 reps (or 4 to 6)
4.	Stimulation (vertical pull) exercise	4-5 sets of 6 to 8 reps (or 4 to 6)
5a.	Potentiation +	3-4 sets of 6-8 reps
5b.	Stimulation + Metabolic	3-4 sets of 6 to 8 reps (or 4 to 6)
5c.	(vertical push) giant set	3-4 sets of 20-30 seconds

Bonus section
Isometric training

Introduction

Isometric literally means "*same length*". So when it comes to resistance training, isometric refers to an exercise where the muscle produces force without changing its length. In other words you're exerting force against a source of resistance, but there is not external movement (the muscle length and joint angle stays the same). There are several ways of utilizing this type of training, which we will see in a few minutes. But first let me explain to you some of the benefits of isometrics and why I personally like to use this type of training.

Benefits of isometric exercises

1. Isometric strength; the capacity to produce force during a static muscle action, is higher than concentric (lifting) strength. In most individuals isometric strength is 10-15% higher than concentric strength (Schmidtbleicher, 1995). This high force production can be used to spark positive neural adaptations that can lead to a significant increase in strength. Remember that the more force you produce, the more high-threshold motor units you must recruit. So in that regard isometric exercises can be useful to stimulate strength and size gains.

2. In most individuals more HTMUs are recruited during a maximal isometric action than during a regular lifting movement. This is especially true in beginners. In that regard isometric exercises can be used to develop the nervous system's capacity to recruit these HTMUs. As your CNS becomes more efficient at recruiting HTMUs during isometric actions, its overall capacity to tap into these powerful fibers will also increase; as a result you will eventually become more efficient at recruiting HTMUs in regular lifting movements. More HTMUs recruited equals more muscle growth and greater strength gains.

3. Isometrics can be used as a potentiating method. I already briefly explained what is potentiation (making a movement more efficient with a previous muscle activity). Potentiation can either be stimulated by explosive movements (which we saw earlier) and by maximal voluntary contraction. The later being called "post-tetanic potentiation". The

tetanus refers to a state of muscular activation that occurs either during a long muscular contraction (so brought on by muscular fatigue) or a very intense contraction (so brought on by a maximum contraction). The tetanus can be explained as the summation of all the available motor-units.

It has been found that the force of the twitch of a muscle fiber is more important after than before the brief tetanus. This effect is present even 5 minutes after the tetanus (O'Leary et al. 1997, Gullich and Schmidtbleicher 1995). In fact, during a 7 second tetanus, the capacity to apply force decreases by 15% <u>while this capacity is increased by 28% after 1 minute, 33% after 2 minutes and 25% after 5 minutes</u> (O'Leary et al. 1997). So it appears that the capacity to produce force is greater 2-3 minutes after the cessation of the tetanic effort.

This increase in the capacity to produce force after a certain stimulation is called post-tetanic potentiation (PTP). The most effective way to promote a large PTP is to place an intense stimulation on a muscle via a maximal effort/maximal tension contraction for a length of 5-10 seconds (Brown and von Euler, 1938, Vandervoort et al. 1983).

PTP can increase contraction strength, especially in fast-twitch fibers (Bowman et al. 1969, Standeart, 1964). PTP also improves the rate of force development (Abbate et al, 2000). So it can be used to potentiate both heavy lifting and explosive movements (Gullich and Schmidtbleicher 1997).

PTP works by increasing the phosphorylation of the myosin light chains, which makes the actin-myosin more sensitive to calcium in the subsequent twitch (Grange et al. 1993, Palmer and Moore 1989, O'Leary et al. 1997). This is not chiefly important, but, if you wish, you can grab a physiology textbook and review the sliding filament theory of muscular contraction to see how this would increase the capacity to produce force.

So to make a long story short, maximal isometrics would seem to be the best way to take advantage of the PTP phenomenon for two reasons:

   a) The force production is higher during an isometric action. More force produced equals greater potentiation.

   b) Isometric movements are less tiring than concentric/regular exercises. As a result potentiation (which improves performance) is increased while fatigue (which decreases performance) isn't significantly elevated. The end result being a greater improvement in force production potential.

To take advantage of this method you should perform a 5-10 seconds maximal isometric action (of an overcoming nature) 2-3 minutes prior to a heavy (or explosive) set of a regular exercise. This potentiating effect can be used to further increase strength, power and size gains. Later we will see what type of isometric method to use for that purpose.

4. Isometric exercises can be used to strengthen a weak point in a lift. The strength gained from isometric exercise is "angle specific" meaning that you increase strength mostly at the angle being trained (there is a 15 degrees carryover). This can both be seen as a limitation and benefit. A limitation in that to strengthen the whole range of motion you must train at least 3 joint angles per movement. But the benefit is that isometrics can be used to strengthen a specific point in a movement's range of motion (sticking point). For example if your bench press sticking point is at the mid-range of the concentric portion, you can utilize isometric work at that specific position to strengthen that weak point without significantly increasing fatigue or increasing the required post-workout recovery time.

5. Isometric strength is important for several athletic actions. For example every movement that requires the athlete to hold a pre-determined body position (e.g. alpine skiing's bent knees position) requires great isometric strength. Actions where there is a rapid switches from eccentric to concentric (running, changes of direction, etc.) also need

isometric strength since before the switch can occur, the resistance must be stopped and that requires both eccentric and isometric strength.

6. Maximum intramuscular tension is attained for only a brief period in dynamic exercises (mostly due to the fact that the resistance has velocity and acceleration components), while in isometric exercises you can sustain that maximal tension for a longer period of time. For example, instead of maintaining maximum intramuscular tension for 0.25 to 0.5 second in the concentric portion of a dynamic movement, you may sustain it for around 3-6 seconds during an isometric exercise. Strength is greatly influenced by the total time under maximal tension. If you can add 10-20 seconds of maximal intramuscular tension per session, then you increase your potential for strength and especially size gains.

As you can see properly applied isometric training can serve many purposes: it can be used to increase strength, power, muscle growth and athletic performance. Since it's much less energy costly than regular lifting, it's also a good way to maintain strength during a season without causing undue fatigue that might lead to a decrease in performance on the field of play.

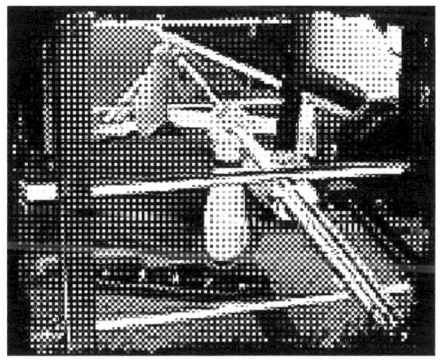

Key points

1. Isometric work can help you improve the capacity to recruit HTMUs over time, especially in beginners and individuals with an inefficient CNS.

2. Isometric exercises are characterised by a high level of force production which can be used to stimulate HTMUs into growth and strengthening.

3. You can use isometric movements to potentiate (make more effective) regular lifting exercises by performing a maximal isometric contraction lasting 5-10 seconds, 2-3 minutes prior to your regular lifting set.

4. If you have a specific weak point in a certain lift, you can rely on isometric exercises performed at that sticking point to correct the problem.

5. Isometric work is much less energy-costly than regular lifting; it won't cause much muscle damage either.

6. Several athletic actions require isometric strength. It's especially important for individuals participating in sports where a fixed body position is used or where frequent changes of direction are required.

Types of isometric work

You'll notice that I will mention three main types of isometric exercises: *overcoming-isometric, yielding-isometric and functional isometrics*. Understand that in the first two cases this doesn't mean that you are combining a concentric/overcoming or eccentric/yielding action along with the isometric action. The actual external outcome of the exercise is the same; there is no movement at all. However, the **intent** during the exercise changes.

Overcoming-isometric: You are pushing or pulling against an immovable resistance. There is no external movement, but your *intent* is to move the resistance (even though it's impossible).

Here you can see the three training positions for the squat in the overcoming-isometric method.

Overcoming-isometrics can also be done against a manual resistance. In the example illustrated to the left coach Thibaudeau is putting bodybuilder Sebastien Cossette through a set of overcoming-isometric lateral raise.

Yielding-isometric: You are holding a weight and your objective is to prevent it from moving down. So once again, there is no external movement. However, your intent is no longer to move the resistance, but to stop its movement.

Below you can see three types of yielding-isometrics: a) holding a barbell, b) supporting your bodyweight plus a dumbbell and c) supporting your body weight.

It is important to understand that both techniques will <u>not</u> have the same effect. For one thing, the neural patterns used in both cases will be different. Overcoming-isometrics may have a bigger impact on concentric strength than yielding-isometrics.

Normally we use overcoming-isometrics for short sets (5-10 seconds) in order to produce a lot of force and stimulate the HTMUs as much as possible.

Yielding-isometrics are utilised mostly for longer sets (20-30 seconds) and have a greater effect on size and strength-endurance than strength.

A third type of isometric work can be added: <u>functional isometrics</u>. These are not 100% isometric in its purest sense since there is some movement involved, but for the most part it is considered an isometric method. Of all the three major methods this one is probably the most effective to stimulate strength gains. It's also much easier to measure progress in this method that with regular overcoming-isometrics, which makes it more motivating.

Functional-isometrics combine a very short range of motion concentric (lifting) action with a maximum overcoming isometric action. It requires the use of a power rack and two sets of safety pins. The bar is set between the two sets of pins (it sits on the first/bottom set of pins in the starting position) and is loaded with a heavy weight. There is 2-4" between both sets of safety pins. The exercise consists of lifting the bar off of the first set and drive it into the second set of pins. Once the bar hits the second set, you push (or pull depending on the movement) against the pins for 5-10 seconds. The differences between this type of training and the regular overcoming-isometrics are that ...

a) There is some concentric/lifting movement involved, even though the range of motion is fairly short.

b) You add weight to the exercise. With regular overcoming isos you simply push/pull an empty bar against the pins while in the functional variation you use a loaded barbell. You keep adding weight to the bar until you reach a load that you cannot hold for 5 seconds against the second set of pins. This makes the exercise more motivating and progress easier to measure.

Below is an illustration of how to set up the rack for some functional isometric work (example for the bench press).

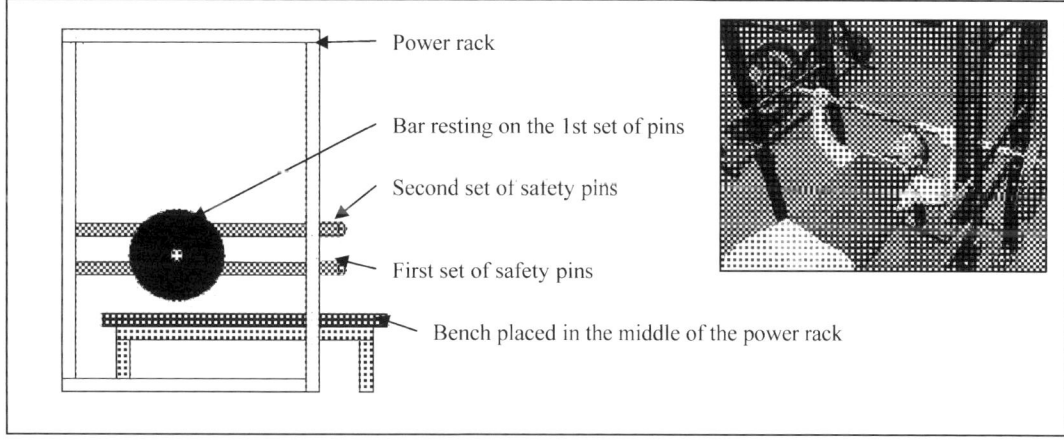

Combo isometric methods

The preceding three isometric methods can be considered "pure iso methods" in that only the isometric action is emphasized. However it is also possible to combine isometric, concentric and eccentric actions in the same exercise/set. These are known as "combo methods".

Combo method 1: Single contrast - yielding

In this method you include one isometric pause during the performance of the eccentric phase of a regular lifting movement. For example in the bench press you would lower the bar down to 2-3" from the chest, hold it there for 3-5 seconds, then lower it down to the chest and lift it back up to the starting position.

Combo method 2: Single contrast – overcoming

In this method you also include a single isometric action, but this time during the lifting phase. And you execute this pause not by simply holding the weight in place, but rather by having a partner push on the bar to stop it. When he does so, you push as hard as you can against this added source of resistance for 3-5 seconds, after which he releases the bar and let you complete the lifting movement.

Combo method 3: Multiple contrast - yielding

This is similar to the first method, however instead of stopping only once during the eccentric portion of the movement you stop 2-5 times (at different positions) for 3-5 seconds.

Combo method 4: Max fatigue contrast

In this method you perform a regular lifting set to muscle failure. When you reach that point you hold the weight for as long as you can. Depending on the type of movement you will hold the weight either at the fully contracted position or at the mid-range point.

Position of the pause depending on the exercise type	
Peak contraction (end of concentric phase)	Mid-range point (middle portion of the range of motion)
Lat pulldown and variations	Bench press and variations
Seated rowing and variations	Dumbbell press and variations
Barbell rowing and variations	Shoulder press and variations
Dumbbell rowing and variations	Squat and variations
Upright rowing and variations	Leg press
Shrugs and variations	Hack squat
Leg extension	Biceps work with barbells
Leg curl	Biceps work with dumbbells
Calf raises and variations	Triceps work with barbells
Lateral raises and variations	Triceps work with dumbbells
Back extension	Deadlift and variations
Triceps work at pulley station	
Biceps work at pulley station	
Cable cross-over	
Pec Deck machine	
Flies at pulley station	

Combo method 5: Potentiation contrast

This isn't really a combo method as the isometric and concentric exercises are separated by 2-3 minutes. However since it makes use of both types of actions I still decided to include it in the combo section. In this method the isometric exercise is used to potentiate the regular lifting exercises. To do so your perform a maximum overcoming-isometric (or functional isometric) action lasting 5-10 seconds, rest for 2-3 minutes, then perform a set of regular lifting. You can either use the isometric action at the sticking point, to potentiate this specific portion of the movement so that it will become a less problematic area or perform the isometric action at the strongest point of the range of motion to have a maximal potentiation effect on the whole movement. Below is illustrated this type of training applied to the bench press.

Max contraction lasting 5-10 seconds

Regular lifting exercise (either heavy weights or explosive)

2-3 minutes rest

As we saw earlier, the type of exercises in which potentiating isometrics have the greatest effect are either heavy or explosive lifts. The more a movement relies on the HTMUs, the more benefits there will be from using potentiating isometrics.

When to use isometrics

Many coaches believe that isometric exercises should be used at the end of a workout (Brunner and Tabachnik 1990, Vorobiev 1988). However, Siff and Verkhoshansky (1999) state that isometric action training can be used first in a workout to potentiate/facilitate subsequent strength and speed-strength exercises. I think that both options can be used: if you are using isometrics to potentiate the main exercise(s), then use it early in a workout, if you are using it to strengthen a weak point or to increase strength/size, then perform it at the end of the session.

Isometrics limitations

It is important to note that isometric action training still has limited applications for an athlete or bodybuilder. Yes, it can help increase strength and size. But without a concurrent dynamic (yielding and overcoming) program the gains will be slow. In other words, don't expect huge gains if you only perform isometric exercises. Schmidtbleicher states that isometric work should comprise around 10% of the training volume when it's used. Some coaches noted that gains from isometric exercise stops after 6-8 weeks of use (Medvedyev 1986). So while isometric action training can be very helpful to work on a weak point or improve an athlete's capacity to activate motor-units, it should only be used for short to medium periods of time when progress has slowed down or when a rapid strength improvement is needed.

Isometric action training can also be useful during periods of lowered training volumes, i.e. when one has to decrease his training load either due to fatigue symptoms or time constraints. In that context isometric work can help prevent muscle and strength losses.

Key points

1. Overcoming-isometrics are more effective when used for short duration (5-10 seconds) at a maximum force of contraction. They are thus better suited to increase strength rather than size.

2. Yielding-isometrics are more effective when used for longer (20-30 seconds) periods of time. They thus better suited to increase muscle growth.

3. Functional isometrics offer the same benefits as OI but with an added motivation factor and it's better to evaluate progress.

4. You can use isometrics at the beginning of the workout to potentiate the main exercise, or at the end of the workout if using them to correct a weak point or stimulate muscle growth.

Parting words

As you probably noticed this book doesn't give you a cookie-cutter program. Rather it's written in a way to teach you the principles and methods that will allow you to design your own super effective training programs. "Give a man a fish and you'll feed him for one day; teach him how to fish and you'll feed him for a lifetime"! I've always believed in education rather than in giving away a dogmatic answer that comes from nowhere.

What's written on a piece of paper is much less important than the basic principles underlying the program and the effort provided in the gym. This is what I was trying to accomplish when I wrote this book: to give you all the tools necessary to allow you to design countless training programs, all leading to special results! In that sense I didn't hand out one workout to you, but a lifetime's worth of workouts! It's now up to you to make the most out of it.

Cool Tools
Equipment, Performance Store and Products that Coach Thib likes

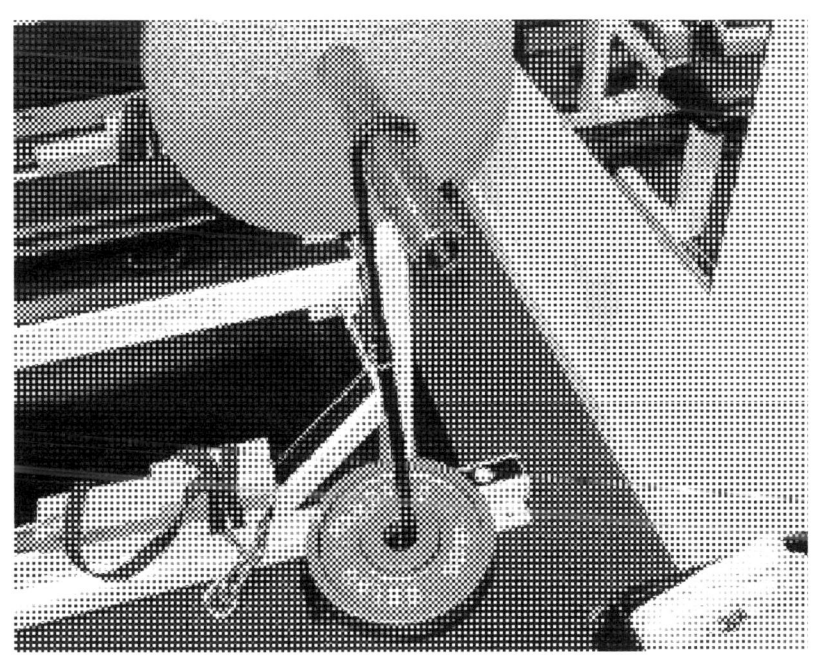

design the perfect diet -- for you.

The Precision Nutrition System.

Introducing Precision Nutrition, the nutrition system used by elite athletes and recreational athletes worldwide to build lean, muscular, high-performance physiques in record time.

* Includes 5 guidebooks, audio lessons, video seminars and the Gourmet Nutrition cookbook.

* Learn to build your own custom tailored nutrition plans for sport performance, fat loss & muscle gain.

* Learn to test & tweak your plan for consistent progress.

To achieve extraordinary results, you need a great training program. But you also need a great nutrition plan -- one that's perfectly tailored to you and your specific needs.

After all, generalized diets, even good ones, don't take into account your unique body type, your unique starting point, and your unique goals. Yet it's attention to those very details that will determine your success or failure. It's learning how to tailor and optimize your nutrition plan. It's individualization. That's what yields exceptional results. And that's what we do at Precision Nutrition.

We teach individualization. We teach you the principles behind the high performance diets we design for Olympic, professional, and collegiate athletes. We teach you the principles behind the advanced fat loss and muscle building diets we design for our professional bodybuilders, models, and fitness competitors. And most importantly, we teach you how to apply and individualize those principles so that they can work for you.

Now understand, it won't be easy. But if you're willing to supply the effort, we'll supply the knowledge. If you want to perform better, feel better, and look better than ever before, we can show you how.

Come find out more online.

John M. Berardi, Ph.D.
President, Precision Nutrition

www.precisionnutrition.com
THE SYSTEM THE PROS TURN TO ™

WELCOME TO THE TYLERGRIP REVOLUTION

INTRODUCING THE TYLERGRIP — A REVOLUTIONARY TRAINING TOOL THAT BUILDS UNSURPASSED GRIP, FOREARM, AND BICEPS STRENGTH!

ABOUT THE TYLERGRIP

The TYLERGRIP is a groundbreaking product based upon the simple biomechanical fact that a closed fist produces maximum gripping power. As the fist opens it makes it more difficult for the fingers to hold and control a given weight.

The TYLERGRIP is a flexible urethane sleeve designed for use with standard weight training equipment. The grips are made from specially molded, solid, heavy duty urethane (**not** foam rubber!) and each grip weighs 8 ounces. The ergonomic cone-shaped design forces the hand open, forcing increased grip strength to keep the fingers closed around the grip. As a result, the TYLERGRIP fatigues the fingers, hands, forearms, and biceps more quickly and more thoroughly, without any increase in the number of sets or time spent working out!

The TYLERGRIP will benefit anyone who trains with weights. If your sport is bodybuilding or tennis, golf or powerlifting, use of the TYLERGRIP will produce immediate strength gains.

BENEFITS

Strongman competitors, powerlifters, and other strength athletes use specially made thick-handled dumbbells and barbells to train for strength, size, and thickness in their forearms and biceps.

The TYLERGRIP improves upon this equipment due to the patent-pending cone-shaped design, which fits the palm of the hand. The solid urethane grips also "give" slightly to the pressure of the fingers and palm giving a rock solid grip. The grips fit most standard weight training equipment allowing variety in weight training exercises. The cost of the TYLERGRIP is only a small fraction of what the thick-handled equipment sells for.

The TYLERGRIP is made to last a lifetime and should never wear out due to normal use. All the maintenance the rugged TYLERGRIP requires is an occasional wash with soap and water.

LEARN MORE ABOUT THE TYLERGRIP AND ORDER ONLINE AT WWW.TYLERGRIP.COM!

Made in the USA
Lexington, KY
13 September 2014